Einst

anu Ramana Maharshi

Reality, Morality, God and Religion

Wasyl Nimenko

Wasyl Nimenko

Goalpath Books

Published by Goalpath Books 2025

Einstein and Ramana Maharshi
Reality, Morality, God and Religion

ISBN 978-1-908142-90-0

Design - Goalpath Books

Albert Einstein photograph 1947 - Orren Jack Turner
Ramana Maharshi photograph 1946 - Gajanan Govind Welling

Wasyl Nimenko was born in Ipswich, England. His mother was from Tubbercurry in the west of Ireland, his father from Dnipro in central Ukraine. After studying medicine in London from 1974-1979, Nimenko began training and working as a psychiatrist. He worked at the 2,200 bed St Bernard's Hospital *(previously known as the 'Hanwell Insane Asylum' and the 'Hanwell Pauper and Lunatic Asylum')* but left psychiatry because of the overemphasis on the chemical causes and treatments of mental health problems.

He left psychiatry to train as a GP and a psychotherapist. From 1982 - 1991 Nimenko worked with survivors of torture. He worked independently, in the NHS, with the homeless and also with the emergency services and the armed forces.

In 1984 Nimenko researched the stress of using virtual reality for Xerox among the first users of the Xerox Star, technology which has since become the standard in personal computers. In 2011 he carried out research into the use of archaeology in the psychological decompression of wounded soldiers, a service which is now available internationally to the armed forces as 'Operation Nightingale.' In 2013 he researched Post Repatriation Stress Disorder which was first described in 2015.

Although Nimenko worked in medicine and psychotherapy in the UK he was also influenced by living in India, New Zealand and Australia. His main interest and practice is in uncovering, recognising and realising our natural happiness.

ALSO BY WASYL NIMENKO

Non-Fiction

Uncovering and Recognising Awareness
Removing our Delusion of Separateness
Do you need a Doctor, Therapist or Guru?
The Spiritual Nature of Addictions
Carl Jung and Ramana Maharshi
Acceptance and Meaning in Grief
Notes from the Inside

Fiction

Invisible Bullets

Travel

Searching in Secret India
Searching in Secret New Zealand and Australia
Searching in Secret Orkney

Poems

The Fool's Poems Part I
The Fool's Poems Part II

CONTENTS

Introduction

Part One: Einstein

Part Two: Ramana Maharshi

Part Three:

Introduction

Do you think there is a force behind the order and laws of nature and everything in the universe? Do you feel with utter conviction that you are aware of a vastly superior intelligence?

Einstein and Ramana Maharshi felt both of these things with certainty. Einstein had a sceptic's curiosity which was transformed into awe when he perceived the unfathomable vastly superior intelligent force behind nature's laws. He also believed in predeterminism in that "We all dance to a mysterious tune, intoned in the distance by an invisible player."

Ramana Maharshi, who Carl Jung described as 'the whitest spot in a white space,' also experienced both with certainty. He lived for 54 years in silence and stillness on a mountain and described how to transcend the personal 'I' to become aware of the oneness of the eternal 'I-I'.

Einstein's understanding of the connections and laws of nature, though incomplete, left him in 'awe' of the superior intelligence behind them. Ramana Maharshi's realisation of the 'Self' left him permanently in a state of blissful stillness.

What follows is not intended to be a detailed scholarly account of Albert Einstein's and Ramana Maharshi's lives or of the contributions they made to their fields of knowledge. The aim is to show their understanding and experiences of reality, morality, God, and religion so that the reader can compare and contrast them with their own understanding and experiences.

The use of mathematics and physics has been largely omitted because they are unnecessary to understand Einstein's conclusions derived from his conceptual, imaginative thinking. He speaks directly and simply and his conclusions need little explanation.

The study of our own mind by psychology is also considered to be of little help to understand what is being sought after because our nature and purpose are ultimately beyond the confines of language. This limitation of understanding by the intellect also applies to other disciplines of the mind such as philosophy and theology.

Crucially, like Aristotle, both Einstein and Ramana Maharshi believed that everything we do is motivated by happiness:

"Happiness is the meaning and purpose of life, the whole aim and end of human existence."

Aristotle

"Why does the desire for happiness arise? Because your nature is happiness itself and it is natural that you come into your own."

Ramana Maharshi

"Everything that men do or think concerns the satisfaction of the needs they feel or the escape from pain."

Albert Einstein

∞

PART ONE

Einstein

1.

Opposite Sides of the Same Coin

Albert Einstein and Ramana Maharshi were born in the same year nine months apart, Einstein in Germany on March 14th, 1879, Ramana Maharshi in South India on 30th December 1879.

They had similar religious upbringings in that they were both brought up in their traditional family religion, Einstein in Judaism and Ramana Maharshi in Hinduism. However, they both had their childhood education in Christian schools. They both dropped out of school in their mid teens.

Einstein primarily used imaginative conceptual thinking to discover and develop his understanding of the force behind the order and laws of nature and everything in the universe. He used almost no mathematics in developing his new theories. Without using religious scripture, Ramana Maharshi practiced his method of 'Self-enquiry' [self knowledge] to understand the nature of consciousness as a direct path to experience awareness of Truth.

Einstein was awarded the 1921 Nobel prize for physics and he travelled the world giving lectures about his view of the Universe. His name is synonymous with genius and he became world famous as one of the most influential scientists.

Ramana Maharshi was described by the Swiss Psychiatrist Carl Jung as, 'the whitest spot on a white surface,' [1] and is regarded as the most important 20th Century guru of consciousness. He is hardly known except by those few interested in the happiness of 'Self-realisation.' He remained in silence in the same place he moved to when he was sixteen until his death. He maintained that his example of silence and stillness were more influential than travelling and lecturing.

In many aspects their life's work could not have been more different, one exploring the measurable reality of the outer Universe, the other enquiring into the truth of our inner nature, and then just being.

It is notoriously difficult to perceive reality. This is because our consciousness is part of reality such that subject and object are inseparable. Furthermore, it is impossible to ascertain whether our reality is the same for other people. Einstein and Ramana Maharshi both invoked consciousness to understand reality. For both of them it is consciousness which validates their sense of a power inherent in the universe. This will become clearer in the chapter on Truth.

They did have two important things in common of which they were certain. The first was they believed in a cosmic God, not in an anthropomorphic God. The second was they believed that everything is predetermined.

Einstein's scientific genius is familiar to most readers, so little explanation is necessary. Although he is less well known for his views on religion and reality, he is such a clear and communicative writer that his words on the subject speak for themselves and need little explanation.

Ramana Maharshi's practice of Self-enquiry, cannot be assimilated and understood as factual knowledge. The only way to understand Self-enquiry is to participate in it because it is solely concerned with experiential learning.

Unlike Einstein's external reality, Ramana Maharshi's reality can only be understood as an 'internal' experience because it is about being aware of what the Self is and recognising as illusory what is "non Self".

There is no intention to Favour Einstein's or Ramana Maharshi's views of God, religion, reality and the Universe. Einstein wrote a great deal, publishing more than 150 non-scientific papers. His views and beliefs can be understood from quotations from his own words.

However, because understanding Ramana Maharshi's Self-enquiry requires actually practicing it, it is described in his own words at more length so that the reader can try and find out about it experientially.

These were two extraordinary men. There is no intention to flatter them with excessive admiration as in a hagiography. This is hopefully prevented by showing how their lives and ideas were constantly being challenged.

The aim is to illustrate Einstein's and Ramana Maharshi's understanding and experiences. The reader can then compare and contrast these with their own understanding and experiences.

Only occasionally is there juxtaposition of these two extraordinary men. This is to highlight some of their most interesting similarities and differences.

First, let us look at Einstein's life, his views on reality, morality, God and religion. Then let us turn to Ramana Maharshi.

2.

The First Awakening - Max Talmey

When Einstein was ten years old, he met Max Talmey, a Jewish medical student from Lithuania, who attended a weekly family meal at Einstein's parents' home for five years. His parents followed a Jewish custom of offering a weekly meal to a poor student. Max Talmey became Einstein's tutor and close friend and lent him several books on mathematics, science and philosophy including Immanuel Kant's *Critique of Pure Reason*. The friendship played a part in changing Einstein's view of religion permanently.

From this time onwards Einstein no longer believed in an anthropomorphic God. Ironically, it seems likely that as a consequence of this friendship, due to his family's only religious custom, he became irreligious and declined being bar mitzvahed.

Although this ceremonious act, introduced in the thirteenth century, is not a "halachist" [necessary] condition for membership in the Jewish community, even liberal Jews regard it as a precept that must be obeyed. By not complying with it, Einstein obviously intended to demonstrate his personal independence from traditional authority [1]

This friendship along with exposure to mathematics, science and philosophy made him start to rely on his own thinking to find out about reality, truth, religion, God and the external Universe. His external searching had begun. He describes this in "Autobiographical Notes" in *'Albert Einstein: Philosopher-Scientist'* as follows:

"As the first way out there was religion, which is implanted in every child by way of the traditional education-machine. Thus I came - despite the fact that I was the son of

5

entirely irreligious [Jewish] parents – to a deep religiosity, which, however, found, an abrupt ending at the age of 12. Through the reading of popular scientific books I soon reached the conviction that much in the stories of the Bible could not be true. The consequence was a positively fanatic orgy of freethinking coupled with the impression that youth is intentionally being deceived by the state through lies; it was a crushing impression. Suspicion against every kind of authority grew out of this experience, a sceptical attitude towards the convictions which were alive in any specific social environment-an attitude which has never again left me, even though later on, because of a better insight into the causal connection, it lost some of its original poignancy." [2]

At twelve years old, Einstein's refusing to be bar mitzvahed marked the turning away not only from organised religion's rituals but also his turning away from all authority. It was only the beginning of his freethinking. As he said:

"Suspicion against every kind of authority grew out of this experience."

This suspicion was to develop into a lifelong personal and moral compass. His initial suspicion of the authority of organised religion widened to include a suspicion of mechanical leaning, military force and nationalism as well as accepted scientific knowledge.

3.

The Second Awakening - School

In 1884, Einstein left his school, the Luitpold-Gymnasium in Munich, where he was very uncomfortable and joined his parents, who having left Munich, were now in Milan, before he started at the Zurich Polytechnical School. [1] In his 1972 book, *The Dynamics of Creation*, Anthony Storr, an English psychiatrist, commented on Einstein's adolescence:

"We do not know whether he ever found the world meaningless or futile: but he certainly went through a mental upheaval at the age of sixteen which was severe enough to enable him to obtain a letter from the school doctor stating that he had a nervous breakdown and must take six months off school. It seems highly probable that part of the motivation of his intense desire to create originated from his lack of close contact with other people, and the consequent idea of finding the world devoid of meaning." [2]

I was surprised by Storr's use of the term 'nervous breakdown' for Einstein's school experience, especially as I could not find any reference to Einstein having a nervous breakdown whilst at the Luitpold-Gymnasium in Munich. I wrote to the Luitpold-Gymnasium in Munich to see if they had a sick note written by Einstein's family doctor. They did not reply. I also wrote to the Einstein Archive to ask if they knew of Einstein having had a nervous breakdown. This was the archivist's reply:

"There is no historical evidence that details a medically diagnosed breakdown or the issuance of such a certificate. Therefore, the account may be speculative or interpretive, aiming to align Einstein's life story with Antohny Storr's book's theme of creative development stemming from personal adversity."

I also wrote to Princeton University Press who manage the

Collected Papers of Albert Einstein. The 'Einstein Papers' showed that he was so uncomfortable at school that he became depressed and nervous. This culminated when he was told by the teacher in charge of his class that 'he would not amount to anything.' He then obtained a sick note from his family doctor. The accessible online Digital Einstein Papers did not say whether the sick note was for a 'nervous breakdown.' [3]

The Einstein Archive could of course be correct about Storr being speculative or interpretive. However, Anthony Storr taught me for a short time in the early 1980's, when I was training as a psychiatrist in Oxford. I suspect Storr may have overidentified with Einstein's experience of being badly treated at school because of his own terrible school experience and his mental health problems.

Storr was bitterly unhappy at school and he suffered bouts of depression all of his life. [4] It was thought then that Storr had been "broken" at Winchester College, one of England's oldest public schools. Winchester College has a long documented history of child abuse dating back to 1872. [5] In 2024 the Archbishop of Canterbury, Justin Welby, resigned because of the 'Makin Review.' [6] This disclosed Welby's failure to investigate or report his known abuse of children by the barrister, John Smythe, who, while running evangelical Christian camps, carried out sadomasochistic abuse on many children, including many of the Winchester College pupils in the 1970s and 80s, which also went unreported until 2022. [7] [8]

During his adolescence, Einstein became strongly opposed to authority because of its reliance on conventional knowledge and commonplace beliefs. This was almost certainly firmly backed up by his utter disillusionment with authority after being treated horribly by a schoolteacher whom he had expected to educate and nurture him.

As an example, Walter Isaacson reports in his biography of

Einstein, *'Einstein-His Life and Universe'*, that when Einstein said he had done nothing wrong, the teacher replied:

"Yes, that is true, but you sit there in the back row and smile, and your mere presence here spoils the respect of the class for me." [9] [10]

Einstein had the intelligence to see a simple way out of this intolerable situation by medicalising it in the form of a doctor's certificate which he obtained from Max Talmey's older brother, Bernard, who was also a medical doctor. [11]

Later we will see that because of his awakening experience of Self-realisation, Ramana Maharshi also left school around 16 years old. He travelled to the mountain, Arunachala, where he lived for the rest of his life. He said that he was rescued from the pain of miserable mundane life.

At just 16 years old, both he and Einstein were transformed and awakened to the certainty of their independence. Their understanding of the basis of reality, human existence and God began to be forged from this time. Their place of further development was not conventional. They did not fit in.

4.

The Third Awakening - The Olympia Academy

Another great influence on Einstein was the Olympia Academy which began when Einstein was just 21 in 1901, before he began working in the Patent Office in Zurich in 1904. This was a year before Einstein's 'miracle' year of 1905.

The Olympia Academy was formed almost accidentally as a result of Einstein needing money and placing an advert in a local Berne newspaper, offering to give private lessons in physics and mathematics. It was answered by Maurice Solovine, a Romanian philosophy student. They were later joined by Conrad Habicht a former neighbour of Einstein's who had studied mathematics and physics. Einstein joked that he could bring in more money than these lessons by busking with his violin. Other members of the group came and went.

The group called themselves the 'Olympia Academy' and Einstein was voted President. They discussed a wide range of scientific and philosophical subjects, debating late into the night, sustained by food and coffee, whilst annoying Einstein's neighbours. Their discussions sharpened Einstein's ideas and gave him new insights into a broad range of subjects. [1]

Some of the books they read and discussed were Karl Pearson's *The Grammar of Science*, Henri Poincaré's *Science and Hypothesis*, John Stuart Mill's *A System of Logic*, David Hume's *Treatise of Human Nature*, and Baruch Spinoza's *Ethics*. They also discussed their own work. [2]

Einstein was particularly influenced by the Olympia Academy's study and discussions about the Austrian physicist, historian and philosopher, Ernst Mach. Mach used 'thought experiments'. We will see later that this type of conceptual thinking was the hallmark of Einstein's most important contributions to physics. [3]

Perhaps most importantly, Mach's ideas were used by Einstein in the development and construction of the theory of relativity. [4]

The picture formed of young Einstein is of an independent, sceptical and very curious young man who did not respect authority. Much of his youth, beginning with Max Talmey was spent with other similarly bright individuals, learning from them, whilst sharpening and fine tuning his own thinking. [5]

The influence of in depth reading and discussion of a broad range of subjects with members of the Olympia Academy opened up Einstein's imaginative conceptual thinking even further.

From this time onwards, he worked similarly with other people who were like-minded individuals, discussing and developing ideas. These discussions included world peace movements, morality and religion and contributed to the publication of many papers and books.

5.

Disbelief in Free Will

Determinism is the view that all events, including human action, are ultimately determined by causes regarded as external to the will. Predeterminism is the view that all events are determined in advance. Here, for simplicity, we will use the terms determinism and predeterminism interchangeably to indicate disbelief in free will.

Einstein not only shared but lived his life by Spinoza's view of determinism which Spinoza illustrated by the throwing of a stone.

Spinoza asked if the stone had consciousness, what would the stone think while flying through the air? He said it would think it was freely flying through the air, just like humans think they have free will. He said we are aware of our desires but ignorant of the causes which determine them.

Essentially, he said that we think we are under the illusion that we have free will and are in control of what we do when there are many influences on us which we are not aware of.

For example, these influences on us today may include:

Our genetics and epigenetics,
Our physical environment such as where we live,
Our health,
Our psychological state,
Our personality,
Our job,
Our use of substances and medication,
Our emotions,
Our expectations,

Our culture,
Our beliefs,
Our relationships,
Our family,
Our social status,
Our friends and groups,
Our social networks,
Our leisure,
Our social media,
News media
The internet,
Books,
Television,
Music,
Art.

The list could go on and include our financial situation, politics, the state of our country, other countries and our planet.

Even though we think we have free will and choose to do things, there are many things that influence us which we are unaware of.

In October 1929 Einstein gave a revealing interview to G.G. Viereck of the Saturday Evening Post.

" . . . I am a determinist. As such, I do not believe in Free Will. The Jews believe in Free Will. They believe that man shapes his own life. I reject that doctrine philosophically. In that respect I am not a Jew."

"Don't you believe that man is a free agent at least in a limited sense?"

Einstein smiled ingratiatingly. "I believe with Schopenhauer: We can do what we wish, but we can only wish what we must.

Practically, I am, nevertheless, compelled to act— *as if* freedom of the will existed. If I wish to live in a civilised community, I must act on the assumption that man is a responsible being.

"I know that philosophically a murderer is not responsible for his crime, nevertheless I must protect myself from unpleasant contacts. I may consider him guiltless. But I prefer not to take tea with him."

"Do you mean to say that you did not choose your own career, but that your actions were predetermined by some power outside of yourself?"

"My own career was undoubtedly determined, not by my own will, but by various factors, over which I have no control," [1] [2]

Einstein saw free will as being useful to live in society because society makes people act responsibly. That is to say it makes them act *as if* they are responsible, even though they have no choice.

He is saying that he treats someone as being responsible for their actions whilst at the same time believing intellectually that they are not responsible because their action was predetermined. However strange it may appear, because we are also like the stone, part of nature, it seems the same laws of nature apply to us.

Einstein is saying that he believes without any doubt at all that his whole life was predetermined. This may come as a surprise but taking into account his deterministic belief in the cause and effect of everything in nature, it seems not only plausible but also logical.

In the same interview when asked about Henry Ford he spoke about fame, power and predetermination:

"I do not care for money, decorations, titles or distinctions mean nothing to me. I do not crave praise. The only thing that gives me pleasure apart from my work, my violin and my boat, is the appreciation of my fellow workers."

"Your modesty," I remarked, "does you credit."

"No," Einstein replied with a shrug of his shoulders, "I claim credit for nothing. Everything is determined, the beginning as well as the end, by forces over which we have no control. It is determined, for the insect as well as for the star. Human beings, vegetables or cosmic dust, we all dance to a mysterious tune, intoned in the distance by an invisible player." [3]

There is admirable modesty in what Einstein says, which constitutes a rare insight into his humility and how he regarded himself as being of the same nature as an insect or a star.

One of Einstein's main pleasures had always been sailing and one of his idiosyncrasies showed his belief in predetermination and disregard for the threat of death. Although he never learnt to swim, Einstein always refused to carry lifejackets on his sailing-boat.

This is perhaps further evidence that Einstein firmly believed in influences which predetermine everything which he called the invisible player.

When asked if destiny can be conquered Ramana Maharshi answered:

M. There are only two ways to conquer destiny or be independent of it. One is to enquire for whom is this destiny and discover that only the ego is bound by destiny and not the Self, and that the ego is non-existent. The other way is to kill the ego by completely surrendering to the Lord, by realizing one's

15

helplessness and saying all the time: 'Not I but Thou, oh Lord!', and giving up all sense of 'I' and 'mine' and leaving it to the Lord to do what he likes with you. Surrender can never be regarded as complete so long as the devotee wants this or that from the Lord. True surrender is love of God for the sake of love and nothing else, not even for the sake of salvation. In other words, complete effacement of the ego is necessary to conquer destiny, whether you achieve this effacement through Self-enquiry or through bhakti-marga [path of devotion]. [4]

6.

Knowing and Believing

Einstein always said he was a determinist along with Spinoza, the 17th-century Dutch philosopher, who believed everything in nature was governed by the laws of cause and effect as shown by the order of mathematics. Spinoza was excommunicated from the Amsterdam Synagogue.

Spinoza believed organised religions should have no authority in worldly affairs in a democratic state. Like Spinoza, Einstein objected to the teaching of religious rituals and ceremonies. Einstein believed science showed what 'is' and ethics showed what 'should be' and that religion and authority should not be responsible for teaching morality.

Spinoza was a pantheist in that he believed God is the Universe and everything in the universe is God, as opposed to panentheists, who believe that the Universe is a manifestation of God but that God also exists beyond the Universe and is beyond time and space.

Ramana Maharshi's belief in Brahman is more encompassing than pantheism as Brahman is seen as a single reality (non-dual) and that God, Self, the Universe and beyond are one.

Einstein's was sometimes asked to give an account of his beliefs and his views frequently upset religious leaders. He always maintained his belief in Spinoza's God.

In 1925 at the New England Province of College Catholic Clubs of America, Cardinal William Henry O'Connell, Archbishop of Boston, claimed that Einstein's theory of relativity stirred up doubt about God and his creation. He attacked Einstein and accused him of not being a true scientist but a plagiarist and also an atheist.

So concerned by this was a New York rabbi, Herbert Goldstein, that he sent Einstein a request for a return telegram regarding Einstein's belief in God:

"Do you believe in God? Stop. Answer paid 50 words."

Einstein's belief in Spinoza's view that God is in everything is seen in his response of 30 words.

"I believe in Spinoza's God who reveals himself in the orderly harmony of what exists, not in a God who concerns himself with the fates and actions of human beings." [1]

Einstein's view of seeing God in the order of nature and in the world of thoughts did not change with time and he repeated the same explanation in his writing over decades.

Although Einstein's view of God being revealed in the orderly harmony of what exists seems perfectly reasonable, for some individuals it may seem unacceptable for someone to depend on reasoning alone as a way to accept there is a God.

In 1959, four years after Einstein's death, in the BBC interview titled, *'Face to Face with Carl Jung,'* John Freeman asked:

'Do you believe in God?' Jung famously replied:

"Difficult to answer. *I know.* I don't need to believe, I know." [2]

Jung evoked a similar angry reaction to Einstein's statement before him, which upset a lot of people. This may be because there seems to be a tradition for people to "believe" (i.e. have faith) God exists rather than "know" (i.e. experience) God exists.

Maybe this is because members of faith-based religions think scientists and intellectuals have less faith. Perhaps this is simply because these members of faith-based religions feel challenged and even threatened by what they may see as a superior intelligence in scientists and intellectuals. This perceived threat from someone with perhaps a better understanding is probably why Einstein upset those belonging to traditional faith-based religions.

If people's thinking and understanding is that it is more correct to believe there is a God rather than know there is a God, then they are more likely going to disapprove and criticise someone who says they know there is a God.

An important reason for continuing to maintain and teach their members this could be that if people "know" there is a God, then what would be the point having members of "faith" based religions to teach what is already known.

A scientist, intellectual or anyone with their own observations, knowledge and experience may come to the rational conclusion that there is a God and therefore know this. It can seem more nonsensical to say a person who "knows" is wrong than to say a person who "believes" is wrong?

They both agree that they "think" there is a God, only the means by which they reach the same conclusion are different.

7.

The Harmonious Force Behind Nature

Many years later in 1947 Einstein reiterates his endorsement of Spinoza's God in a letter to Marvin Magalaner who was professor of English at the City College of New York.

In reply to your letter of April 10th, I am sending you the following short remarks:

"It seems to me that the idea of a personal God is an anthropomorphic concept and one which I cannot take seriously. I feel also not able to imagine some will or goal outside the human sphere. My views are near those of Spinoza: admiration for the beauty and belief in the logical simplicity of the order and harmony that we can grasp humbly and only imperfectly. I believe that we have to content ourselves with our imperfect knowledge and understanding and treat values and moral obligations as a purely human problem-the most important of all human problems." [1]

Our understanding of Einstein's religious belief becomes clearer and more sharply focused the more we read his many comments. Einstein's comments are whole-heartedly human and are based on reasonable arguments. His refusal to accept reasons based on human frailty while at the same time accepting his knowledge is tempered with emotion make his ideas of God seem even more reasonable. These descriptions are eye-opening as many readers may not have come across them before.

Milton Schayer a Denver businessman wrote to Einstein in 1927 saying most scientists had given up the idea of a personal God such as a bearded benevolent father figure surrounded by angels. He asked for Einstein's views on this pointing out that he had written to other eminent people asking them the same thing and he had so far heard from twenty-four Nobel prize winners. Einstein's response was:

"I cannot conceive of a personal God who would directly influence the actions of individuals or would directly sit in judgement on creatures of his own creation. I cannot do this in spite of the fact that mechanistic causality has, to a certain extent, been placed in doubt by modern science.

My Religiosity consists of a humble admiration of the infinitely superior spirit that reveals itself in the little that we can comprehend of the knowable world. That deeply emotional conviction of the presence of a superior reasoning power, which is revealed in the incomprehensible universe, forms my idea of God." [2]

Einstein humbly recognises the infinitely superior reasoning in a Higher Power which is described in a similar way by Ramana Maharshi.

M. The intellect itself realises after continuous practice that it is enabled by some Higher Power to function. It cannot itself reach that Power. So it ceases to function after a certain stage. When it thus ceases to function the Supreme Power is still left there all alone. That is Realisation; that is the finality; that is the goal. [3]

In 1930 Einstein wrote an article for the American magazine 'Forum and Century' titled "What I believe," stating that he did not believe in a personal rewarding and punishing God.

"I cannot imagine a God who rewards and punishes the objects of his creation, whose purposes are modelled after our own God, in short, who is but a reflection of human frailty. Neither can I believe that the individual survives the death of his

21

body, although feeble souls harbour such thoughts through fear or ridiculous egotism. It is enough for me to contemplate the mystery of conscious life perpetuating itself through all eternity, to reflect upon the marvellous structure of the universe which we can dimly perceive, and to try humbly to comprehend even an infinitesimal part of the intelligence manifested in nature." [4]

Einstein sees God in nature as an extraordinary intelligence which we are not able to understand. He virtually resigns himself to being able only to contemplate God.

A similar view was echoed in 1944 in Florence by Max Planck, the originator of Quantum Physics, a fellow Nobel Prize winner who was both a hero and a friend of Einstein's. He said in a lecture: 'The Nature of Matter:'

"As a man who has devoted his whole life to the most clear-headed science, to the study of matter, I can tell you as a result of my research about atoms this much: There is no matter as such. All matter originates and exists only by virtue of a force which brings the particle of an atom to vibration and holds this most minute solar system of the atom together. We must assume behind this force the existence of a conscious and intelligent spirit. This spirit is the matrix of all matter." [5]

He is saying that an intelligent conscious spirit has to exist behind the force which holds the matrix of everything in the universe together.

This was quite an extraordinary thing to say as it brought physics to a level where it had to assume that a conscious spirit is seen as the ultimate force in the universe.

We will touch on this again when we start to look at the Eastern view of reality.

8.

Acknowledging being a Religious Person.

It is not immediately clear what Einstein believed. His understanding of God was complex partly because it was based on rational appreciation. As we move through his various written descriptions, we will see he was more profoundly religious than is generally thought.

In 1927 Harry Kessler recorded in his diary a conversation over dinner between Alfred Kerr and Einstein. During the conversation Einstein admitted he was a religious person inspired by the force behind nature.

"Try and penetrate with our limited means the secrets of nature and you will find that, behind all the discernible laws and connections, there remains something subtle, intangible, and inexplicable. Veneration for this force beyond anything that we can comprehend is my religion. To that extent I am, in point of fact, religious." [1]

The use of "behind" suggests Einstein is not pantheistic (seeing all is God) but rather panentheistic (seeing God as greater than the universe, than all things, beyond space and time).

Einstein seems to be saying that he has a sense of the intangible in nature and beyond nature which he is not able to explain with logical thought. This could be understood as there being an incomprehensible mystery behind or beyond nature.

Three years later in 1930 Einstein wrote about this in more detail in an article *"What I believe,"* for *'Forum and Century,'* the American magazine on politics and culture.

"The most beautiful thing we can experience is the

mysterious. It is the source of all true art and science. He to whom this emotion is a stranger, who can no longer pause to wonder and stand rapt in awe, is as good as dead: his eyes are closed. This insight into the mystery of life, coupled though it be with fear, has also given rise to religion. To know that what is impenetrable to us really exists, manifesting itself as the highest wisdom and the most radiant beauty which our dull faculties can comprehend only in their most primitive forms – this knowledge, this feeling, is at the center of true religiousness. In this sense, and in this sense only, I belong in the ranks of devoutly religious men." [2]

Einstein is saying that the only explanation for the origin of true art and science remains a mysterious feeling. He boldly describes it as 'this emotion' and goes even further to say that without it we are as good as dead. He admits that it remains incomprehensible but that it exists. He says that knowing this and feeling it is the centre of his religiosity.

This was a pivotal statement. Einstein has both the humility and the courage to admit how little we know while boldly professing a transcendental religious awareness.

This is encouraging and reassuring to many followers of faith-based religions who do not know with certainty that what they regard as God exists. It might also shift some agnostic's knowledge more in the direction of knowing that there is a God. His statement will also be of help to those who are in doubt and also to those who may have lost their conviction that there is some form of higher power.

Between 1954 and 1955, not long before he died, Einstein wrote a draft reply to a letter, but it is not known if it was sent. He corrected a misunderstanding of his use of the word mysticism concerning the place of human intelligence in the Universe. It illustrates how important he thought religious feelings are.

"The misunderstanding here is due to a faulty translation of a German text, in particular the use of the word 'mystical.' I have never imputed to nature a purpose or a goal, or anything that could be understood as anthropomorphic. What I see in nature is a magnificent structure that we can comprehend only very imperfectly, and that must fill a thinking person with a feeling of humility. This is a genuinely religious feeling that has nothing to do with mysticism." [3]

Einstein implies that the structure of nature, and presumably the intelligence supporting it, is beyond our full understanding. This can only leave us to assume that he also had reverential respect for the force behind the awe-inspiring structure of nature. Describing his understanding as a genuine 'religious' feeling can only mean a belief in the Divine.

9.

Levels of Attainment.

In November 1939 an article by Einstein titled *"Religion and Science"* appeared in the New York Times Magazine. In it Einstein considered three different types of religious belief, the last of which was his own belief. These were loosely based on three levels of man's thinking: primitive man, civilised man and gifted individuals or high-minded communities.

Einstein's 'intellectual' understanding of a religious belief resonates with Ramana Maharshi's understanding through different levels of 'awareness,' as we shall see. In the article Einstein wrote:

"With primitive man it is above all fear that evokes religious notions - fear of hunger, wild beasts, sickness, death. Since at this stage of existence understanding of causal connections is usually poorly developed, the human mind creates illusory beings more or less analogous to itself on whose wills and actions these fearful happenings depend. Thus, one tries to secure the favour of these beings by carrying out actions and offering sacrifices which, according to the tradition handed down from generation to generation, propitiate them or make them well disposed toward a mortal. In this sense I am speaking of a religion of fear. This, though not created, is in an important degree stabilized by the formation of a special priestly caste which sets itself up as a mediator between the people and the beings they fear . . . " [1]

In 1938 when Ramana Maharshi was questioned about different levels of experiencing religion, his answers were similar to Einstein's. Ramana Maharshi explained the particular level experienced by a seeker depended on the nature of the mind of each seeker.

26

Q. "Is the experience of the Highest State the same to all? Or is there any difference?"

M. The Highest State is the same and the experience is also the same.

Q. But I find some difference in the interpretations put on the Highest Truth.

M. The interpretations are made with the mind. The minds are different and so the interpretations are different.

Q. I mean to ask if the seers [wise ones] express themselves differently?

M. The expressions may differ according to the nature of the seekers. They are meant to guide the seekers. One seer speaks in the terms of Christianity, another in those of Islam, a third of Buddhism, etc. Is that due to their upbringing? Whatever may be their upbringing, their experience is the same. But the modes of expression differ according to circumstances. [2]

Einstein describes the next level as a social or moral conception of God. This level is a social level above primitive man's understanding. It is based on the elders of larger communities maintaining peace and harmony by establishing rules of what is right and wrong and the consequences of breaking these rules.

"The social impulses are another source of the crystallization of religion. Fathers and mothers and the leaders of larger human communities are mortal and fallible. The desire for guidance, love, and support prompts men to form the social or moral conception of God. This is the God of Providence, who protects, disposes, rewards, and punishes; the God who, according to the limits of the believer's outlook, loves and cherishes the life of the tribe or of the human race, or even life itself; the comforter in sorrow and unsatisfied longing; he

27

who preserves the souls of the dead. This is the social or moral conception of God . . ." [3]

Ramana Maharshi says that many people are simply content with everything being God's will. But he also describes a higher level of man's awareness, which makes him want more information and instructions to live a happier life.

Q. How shall I secure that firm faith?

M. Exactly. It is for such as these who want instructions. There are persons who seek freedom from misery. They are told that God guides all and so there need not be any concern about what happens. If they are of the best type they at once believe it and firmly abide by faith in God. [4]

Finally, Einstein describes the third level, his own concept of religion which he says is rare and is based on the order revealed in nature and in the world of thought.

"Common to all these types is the anthropomorphic character of their conception of God . . . But there is a third stage of religious experience which belongs to all of them, even though it is rarely found in a pure form: I shall call it cosmic religious feeling. It is very difficult to elucidate this feeling to anyone who is entirely without it, especially as there is no anthropomorphic conception of God corresponding to it. The individual feels the futility of human desires and aims and the sublimity and marvellous order which reveal themselves both in nature and in the world of thought. Individual existence impresses him as a sort of prison, and he wants to experience the universe as a single significant whole." [5]

Einstein is expressing our desire to experience an *'awareness of oneness with everything.'* He spent the rest of his life trying to find an answer to the 'Unified Field Theory' which he thought would give us a vital understanding of the Universe. The Unified Field

Theory was an attempt to find a hypothetical singular theoretical framework of physics explaining all the fundamental forces of nature. The answer is still being sought worldwide by many physicists.

Ramana Maharshi's answer to awareness and understanding God and the Universe (the equivalent to Einstein's third highest level of religion) is given in two answers to questions about his method of Self-enquiry

    M. But there are others who are not so easily convinced of the truth of the bare statement. They ask: "Who is God? What is His nature? Where is He? How can He be realised?" and so on. In order to satisfy them intellectual discussion is found necessary. Statements are made, their pros and cons are argued, and the truth is thus made clear to the intellect. When the matter is understood intellectually the earnest seeker begins to apply it practically. He argues at every moment, "For whom are these thoughts? Who am I?" and so forth, until he is well established in the conviction that a Higher Power guides us. That is firmness of faith. Then all his doubts are cleared and he needs no further instructions. [6]

    M. In his attempt to fulfil his desires he extends his vision far and wide and yet he turns away dissatisfied. He now begins to think and reason. The desire for permanency of happiness and of peace bespeaks such permanency in his own nature. Therefore, he seeks to find and regain his own nature, i.e., his Self. That found, all is found. Such inward seeking is the path to be gained by man's intellect. The intellect itself realises after continuous practice that it is enabled by some Higher Power to function. It cannot itself reach that Power. So, it ceases to function after a certain stage. When it thus ceases to function, the Supreme Power is still left there all alone. That is Realisation; that is the finality; that is the goal.

It is thus plain that the purpose of the intellect is to realise its own dependence upon the Higher Power and its inability to reach the same. So, it must annihilate itself before the goal is gained. [7]

10.

Realising Our Inner Nature

When we read Einstein's words about his 'feeling of the sublimity and marvellous order which reveal themselves both in nature and in the world of thought,' it can leave us feeling in awe of what he described as a 'cosmic religious feeling.'

Even if we only have a tenuous grasp of religion and philosophy we can still have reverential respect for a force behind the order and laws of nature and nature itself.

Ramana Maharshi, like Einstein, did not believe in a personal, anthropomorphic God. His God is more in keeping with Brahman in the Vedanta Hindu philosophy.

Brahman is seen as the ultimate universal reality, the cause of everything that exists uniting everything including consciousness as a single binding unity (non-dual reality). Ramana Maharshi believed that the Self and God are one and the same, beyond intellectual understanding. This awareness can be realised only by direct experience.

When we read Ramana Maharshi's words he invites us to look inside ourselves. We find out who we are by finding out what we are not. This cannot be learnt from reading books.

The answer is inside you. It is understood only by experiential learning.

What we may read is only of interest on an intellectual level. It is only by accepting the inner invitation from inside yourself that you can understand the path of Ramana Maharshi.

The reason why we want to know how Einstein and Ramana

Maharshi understood God is that just like them, we want to understand and experience this too.

This is because our strongest desire is our desire for happiness. In order to be happy we need to fully understand who and what we are and also what our purpose in life is. We need to have meaning.

On 2nd October 1938 Ramana Maharshi was asked a question by a visitor:

Q. How shall I overcome my passions?

M. Why does the desire for happiness arise? Because your nature is happiness itself and it is natural that you come into your own. This happiness is not found anywhere besides the Self. Do not look for it elsewhere. But seek the Self and abide therein. Still again, that happiness which is natural is simply re-discovered, so it cannot be lost. Whereas the happiness arising from other objects are external and thus liable to be lost. Therefore, it cannot be permanent and so it is not worth seeking [1]

As we have seen, in the fourth century BCE the Greek philosopher Aristotle wrote:

'Happiness is the meaning and purpose of life, the whole aim and end of human existence.'

In 1930 Einstein wrote on this theme in the New York Times Magazine:

"Everything that men do or think concerns the satisfaction of the needs they feel or the escape from pain. This must be kept in mind when we seek to understand spiritual or intellectual movements and the way in which they develop. For feeling and longing are the motive forces of all human striving and productivity—however nobly these latter may display themselves to us." [2]

11.

Separating Morality from Organised Religion

Einstein thought that moral education should be secular, separate from religion. Morality needs to arise from education and society as a whole. The idea of 'secular morality' is not new and goes back to the ancient Greeks. In an article in the New York Times Magazine in November 1930 Einstein wrote:

"A man's ethical behaviour should be based effectually on sympathy, education, and social ties and needs; no religious basis is necessary. Man would indeed be in a poor way if he had to be restrained by fear of punishment and hopes of reward after death." [1]

Einstein was convinced that priests should give up the whole idea of a personal God and therefore forgo the extensive power it gave them.

"In their struggle for the ethical good, teachers of religion must have the stature to give up the doctrine of a personal God, that is, give up that source of fear and hope which in the past placed such vast power in the hands of priests. In their labours they will have to avail themselves of those forces which are capable of cultivating the Good, the True, and the Beautiful in humanity itself. This is, to be sure, a more difficult but an incomparably more worthy task. After religious teachers accomplish the refining process indicated they will surely recognize with joy that true religion has been ennobled and made more profound by scientific knowledge." [2]

Einstein also found it inconceivable that an omnipotent God should punish or reward His own creation as, in doing so, He would be passing judgment on Himself.

"Nobody, certainly, will deny that the idea of the existence of an omnipotent, just, and omni-beneficent personal God is able to accord man solace, help, and guidance; also, by virtue of its simplicity it is accessible to the most undeveloped mind. But, on the other hand, there are decisive weaknesses attached to this idea in itself, which have been painfully felt since the beginning of history. That is, if this being is omnipotent, then every occurrence, including every human action, every human thought, and every human feeling and aspiration is also His work; how is it possible to think of holding men responsible for their deeds and thoughts before such an almighty Being? In giving out punishment and rewards He would to a certain extent be passing judgment on Himself. How can this be combined with the goodness and righteousness ascribed to Him? [3]

Let us answer Einstein's question, How could God be good and righteous in punishing people? The only honest answer is that a supposedly merciful God would not be good and righteous to punish those who offend him with eternal torment.

If we think transgressors need punishment, then we should take on the responsibility to serve justice ourselves and not in God's name, invoking the Deity as a reason to justify our own moral choices.

Moreover it is now clear that even during Einstein's lifetime, unethical behaviour in religious organisations was commonplace at every level, just as it is today.

Einstein never forgave the German people who were mostly Christian for voting Hitler in as their leader. This resulted in Einstein having to leave his home and country to go into exile in the USA and ultimately led to the Second World War and the mass slaughter of the Holocaust.

On 13 November 1950 a Brooklyn church minister wrote to Einstein regarding a statement he had apparently made about the weak response of the church to events in Nazi Germany up to and during World War Two. Einstein was reported to have said that the universities, newspaper editors, and literary writers who all proclaimed their love of freedom for truth did not speak up about what was happening in Nazi Germany.

The Brooklyn minister quoted Einstein as also having said:

"Only the Church stood squarely across the path of Hitler's campaign for suppressing the Truth. I never had any special interest in the Church before, but now I feel a great affection and admiration because the Church alone has had the courage and persistence to stand for intellectual truth and moral freedom."

Fake news and blatant misrepresentation are clearly not a new phenomenon.

On 14 November Einstein replied:

" . . . Shortly after Hitler came to power in Germany I had an oral conversation with a newspaper man about these matters. Since then my remarks have been elaborated and exaggerated beyond recognition . . . I like yourself am predominantly critical concerning the activities and especially the political activities, through history of the official clergy. [4]

On 16 November the minister replied saying he was glad that Einstein's statement had not been reported correctly and he too had reservations about the role of the Church in World War Two.

On 20 November Einstein replied:

"The most important human endeavour is the striving for the morality in our actions. Our inner balance and even our very existence depend on it. Only morality in our actions can give beauty and dignity to life. To make this a living force and bring it to clear consciousness is perhaps the foremost task of education. The foundation of morality should not be made dependent on myth nor tied to any authority lest doubt about the myth or about the legitimacy of the authority imperil the foundation of sound judgement and action." [5]

Religions today have lost their way. Their popularity is in decline because they fail to deliver what their primary purpose should be. Typically inspired by a founding prophet's transcendental state of experiencing a feeling of *awareness of oneness with everything.* religions originated to show others how to transcend to a state of oneness with everything. By failing to teach how to attain this state, which was their original *raison d'être*, they have outlived the justification for their existence. [6]

In order to maintain their power over people as well as their importance, religions assumed the role of moral arbiter, that is the authority on what is right and wrong, and they also moved into the arena of politics.

In 1950 Einstein repeated that morality should not be linked to any religion or authority. His advice, alas, has repeatedly fallen on deaf ears, as has been testified by widespread institutional corruption.

12.

Morality is more Crucial than Science and Technology

Einstein's awe of what he perceived in nature as a superior intelligence was so great that he dedicated much of his life's later work to understanding it in the form of his elusive Unified Field Theory.

Not only did he spend vast amounts of time in solitude, he also lectured on his findings all over the world, such was the importance he attributed to the superior intelligence he felt was manifest in the natural order and laws in the universe.

However, he also emphasised that humanity needs all its strength to guard and preserve the teachings of the founders of the main religious faiths. Einstein is possibly referring to the new moral insights religious founders originally brought to humanity.

More probably he means the moral code passed on by the prophets, such as the Ten Commandments, which have a role to play amongst the masses, who without the restraints imposed by organised religion might become lawless.

The precise circumstances under which he composed the following 1937 statement are not known.

"Our time is distinguished by wonderful achievements in the fields of scientific understanding and technical application of those insights. Who would not be cheered by this? But let us not forget that knowledge and skills alone cannot lead humanity to a happy and dignified life. Humanity has every reason to place the proclaimers of high moral standards and values above the discoveries of objective truth. What humanity owes to personalities like Buddha, Moses, and Jesus ranks for me higher than all the achievements of the enquiring and constructive mind.

What these blessed men have given us we must guard and try to keep alive with all our strength if humanity is not to lose its dignity, the security of its existence, and joy in living." [1]

Einstein argues that our achievements in science and technology, "impressive as they may seem, are not as important as high moral standards and values in ensuring dignity, happiness and ultimately humanity's survival."

Einstein is emphatic that moral standards in life are vital for man's survival and that it is education's most important task to bring this to our consciousness.

His words are even more important now in these times of great change where children and adults use the internet's virtual reality of artificial intelligence as their 'go to' authority.

It seems we may have already passed the stage where moral education could have been included as a compulsory subject on the curriculum of all schools. Maybe we are approaching the stage where it is necessary for our survival. At this point we may no longer have the luxury of a choice.

13.

The Dehumanising Impact of Technology

In 1946 Einstein wrote to a friend, Dr Otto Juliusburger who was a psychiatrist. In 1937, Juliusburger and his family managed by the skin of their teeth to leave Germany and the increasingly savage anti-Semitic persecution that was taking place there. This was four years before the gas chambers began to be used as industrialised weapons of mass murder.

"I think that we have to safeguard ourselves against people who are a menace to others, quite apart from what may have motivated their deeds. What need is there for a criterion of responsibility? I believe that the horrifying deterioration in the ethical conduct of people today stems primarily from the mechanisation and dehumanisation of our lives - a disastrous byproduct of the development of the scientific and technical mentality. Nostra Culpa? [through our fault] I don't see any way to tackle this disastrous shortcoming. Man grows cold faster than the planet he inhabits." [1]

Einstein was quite right about the cause of the horrifying deterioration of humanity's ethical decline being due to the rise of scientific and technical thinking

Einstein correctly thought that the worst consequences of ethical decline would be the use of weapons of mass destruction such as nuclear weapons. He was also correct in predicting how man would continue to dehumanise within, without any foreseeable way for this to stop.

The dehumanisation of our lives has continued since Einstein's warning about technology in 1946 but the mechanism of how technology alters our moral behaviour has changed and has now infiltrated every nook and cranny of our lives.

When helping is not helping

We were blind to what technology could do to us. Initially we grudgingly accepted it in our lives to assist us in the workplace. After all, it did take some of the drudgery out of our repetitive monotonous work which could now be done faster with the aid of a machine. But we soon became conditioned to accepting technological "progress" in many other areas of our lives.

Because of the benefits they seem to bring, we have become programmed by the machines we use, as well as addicted to them. The main culprit is the smartphone which is not predominantly a phone at all but a small handheld computer with state of the art computer technology.

Smartphones have permeated every country, every age group and every aspect of our lives, yet we continue to ignore the warning signals of their negative effects on our mental health and on our happiness. The hidden long-term downsides of computer technology are at last being gradually recognised.

In response to this alarming development a small but significant alternative movement has recently arisen to promote the use of 'dumb phones.' In 2024, 'dumb phones' which offer phone calls and texting functions only, started to become popular once again.

We may also take heart in the parallel reduction of teenagers' and young adults' consumption of alcohol in the UK. It remains to be seen whether reduced addiction to 'on-line' activities can also be achieved. Schools and parents are advising children, 'If you want to be smart get a dumb phone.'

I have to confess at this point that I am guilty of not being farsighted enough to have predicted these developments. Way back in 1984 I was given the opportunity to identify possible dangers in the use of the new digital technologies.

I failed to predict that this technology would be miniaturised and used by everyone, just as clocks were miniaturised to be used by everyone as personal time pieces in the form of watches. Like so many others I also failed to see the extent to which we would become obsessively dependent on this technology in such a short space of time.

In 1984 there were already concerns that individuals using the latest technology might be having mental health problems. I was asked by Phil Judkins from the Xerox Corporation, to look at the possible psychological effects of using new computer technology and in particular the consequences of immersion in 'virtual reality.'

The computer used in the study was the Star Workstation, officially known as the Xerox 8010. The Star was introduced by the Xerox Corporation in 1981 and was the first computer to incorporate various technologies that have since become standard in personal computers, including a bitmapped display, a window based graphical user interface, icons, folders, mouse (two-button) Ethernet networking, file servers, print servers and e-mail. The Star represented a milestone in the human computer interface which was thought of as a step towards developing virtual reality computer systems.

After discussions with leading IT people of the day, doctors and psychologists, a research study was designed and undertaken by myself and my former teacher, John Heron, the pioneering clinical psychologist. The group consisted of 21 people who were using the Star for eight hours a day.

The subjects were psychologically assessed in depth by John Heron, myself, and a counsellor and a physiotherapist. Physical examination and tests were carried out for physiological effects of stress. Blood pressure and pulse were measured and detailed blood tests carried out for biochemical and hormonal changes associated with stress.

At the end of the research, the unanimous conclusion was that using this technology at work for eight hours a day did not lead to significant stress of any kind. I decided not to publish the research findings. This was because I thought I had found nothing of significance to report.

If the same research were conducted today on a similar group of people, the findings would certainly be different. The main reason for this seems to be that it is not the use of computers in the workplace which has changed us but double use injury and multiple use injury.

Musicians hardly ever injure themselves simply by playing their instruments because as a result of their training they develop the necessary stamina. However, when they also use their hands to do strenuous tasks in their spare time, such as painting ceilings or other manual work, they frequently sustain a 'double use injury' the cause of which may not be immediately clear.

Similarly, the average person whose use of a computer is limited to the working day seems to come to no psychological or physiological harm but when there is obsessive use of other computers, including smartphones and tablets, in the evenings, the result may be 'multiple use fatigue.'

But the dangers do not stop here. We may become addicted to many of the applications of computer technology, such as video games, as we habitually immerse ourselves in virtual worlds.

Overuse or over-immersion in virtual worlds outside of 'working hours' may be encouraged as a normal way of occupying our time, especially by those who benefit from us doing so.

Over-immersion can be an easy escape from the real world of having to interact with family and friends. For some it can initially be an easier way to feel more comfortable experiencing less pain and discomfort than in the real world.

Over-immersion in a virtual world may become our easiest 'default' way of occupying time so that eventually we become self-programmed to plug into this virtual world, over-immersing in it to the point where the virtual world acts like a drug, numbing us like any opiate and enabling us to shun authentic feelings.

As our experience of the real world diminishes, our interaction with other human beings may become almost non-existent.

Although the absence of relating to real people may help us to avoid certain problems, it also deprives us of the potential benefits and nurture offered by human contact.

It is over forty years since the Xerox research project on the Star and we have in that time become proficient at multi-tasking with two or three of these devices at the same time. Today a person may use a laptop, tablet, smart-phone, smart watch, eyeglasses, contact lenses or heads up display (HUDS), as well as noise cancelling headphones to communicate with hundreds or even millions of people by e-mail, Facebook, Facetime, Twitter, Instagram, Snapchat or other electronic formats.

They may use these obsessively at all times of day or night, at work, in education, at home, in intimate relationships, for business, for sex, for religion, for entertainment, as leisure, as therapy or for criminal purposes.

With these devices a funeral can be relayed to absent relatives who may not be able to travel, wherever they may be in the world. And although this in some respects may be seen as progress, it comes with the loss of many things and can lead only to a second-rate reality.

A person attending an e-funeral does not have the same depth of experience as a mourner who travels, meets, greets, holds hands and embraces the bereaved. They cannot share the experience of being there. They cannot smell the flowers or be with the deceased on their last journey. They cannot throw that flower onto the coffin.

The loss of basic experiences is a serious challenge and a threat to mankind, because, by permitting the entry of technology into our lives to help us we may have diminished our range of experience. This reduces not only our understanding but also our feelings about people, places and things. It leads us to behave less autonomously and more like automated machines.

Technology has enabled us to communicate instantly with almost anyone anywhere and at a tiny cost and there have been great advances in access to information, in medicine and travel. But has this apparent progress improved our quality of life? Are we more fulfilled than we were in the pre-digital age?

The extraordinary technology which children have easy access to in order to gather and process information has also unfortunately been used by the media to over-promote competitiveness rather than cooperativeness, greed rather than sharing, power rather than empowering and worship of celebrity status rather than equality.

Computer technology knows exactly where we are, what we are doing and also expects us to respond in real time, therefore pressurising us, controlling us and taking away our freedom.

The amount and type of information we are lured into receiving and interacting with requires our nervous system to act as an obedient machine.

In the past values such as honesty, compassion and humility were promoted and nurtured by parents at home, teachers at school and religious figures in temples and churches. Over the years these parents, teachers and inner guides have been pushed to the side by other things such as psychology, the new age and finally new technologies. We are now in a crisis about our core values which should define us as co-operative, caring, civilised humans. Technology plays a significant role in disrupting this.

Perhaps we are becoming more 'down and out.' Maybe we have been moving downwards as opposed to upwards in that we are not flourishing, we are not thriving, we are less happy, we are unhealthy and generally less fortunate. Our objectives and aspirations are increasingly being directed outwards to external things (more superficial and materialistic) as opposed to turning inwards and experiencing our oneness with everything (more spiritual).

In their advanced training, members of the armed forces, such as air crew and special forces, who are at the highest risk of falling into enemy hands, have to re-learn basic survival skills, such as how to find water, food and shelter, and learn to live whilst hiding and evading capture.

To primitive man the use of these skills was essential. It is ironic that in some of the world's most technologically advanced countries (UK, USA, Canada, Australia and New Zealand) air crew, Special Forces and secret service agents now have to spend weeks learning these essential skills on specialist "Survival, Evasion, Resistance and Escape" (SERE) courses. That it is only the most advanced countries that have to do this is indicative of the fact that technological advance is often accompanied by a loss of fundamental self-reliance.

It is common to overindulge in the use of technology to the point of binge use. We are already at a point where technology substitutes everyday experiences. There are even corporate mindfulness courses online. Already some individuals are having to go on specialised courses to learn how to be in a room with family or friends for prolonged periods without resorting to technology. Some have to go on courses to learn how to be able to have a meaningful intimate relationship. Others have to go on courses to learn how to spend leisure time without technology so that they can relax and psychologically decompress.

If we have to go back to classes to re-learn how to be friends, how to relate to people, how to be gentle and kind and how to enjoy life, then what have we become? We have not yet fully realised the position we are in because the consequences have not been seen or felt on a large enough scale nor made a significant negative impact to make us want to do something about it.

Technology, in the form of simple tools, originally helped mankind to survive. A rock could help fight off an assailant, whether another man or a beast. A rock could also be used in the form of an arrowhead to kill an animal for food. A metal rock changed by heat could be used to cut wood for a timber shelter.

Technology might one day be able to transport us to distant planets to set up new civilisations. It may even enable us to preserve the contents of our brains in a memory device. But it won't be able to mimic and preserve 'our awareness of oneness with everything.'

If it seems easier to relate to the reality of digital devices than to people, many will choose the digital devices. We might ask, 'What is new about mankind being this dependent on technology?'

The answer is that if we program ourselves to do this for long enough, we risk ceasing to be human and becoming enslaved by the very electronic devices that were originally designed to serve us.

We know that our misuse of technology can destroy both us and the planet which nourishes us. Perhaps we will change how we interact with and use technology and take steps to become less dependent on the machines we use. [2]

14.

Intellectual Destruction of human Relationships.

In 1951 Einstein paid tribute to the liberal 'Ethical Culture Society' whose motto was "Deed rather than Creed." A letter from Einstein was read in New York:

"Here no science can save us. I believe, indeed, that overemphasis on the purely intellectual attitude, often directed solely to the practical and factual, in our education, has led directly to the impairment of ethical values. I am not thinking so much of the dangers with which technical progress has directly confronted mankind, as of the stifling of mutual human considerations by the "matter-of-fact" habit of thought which has come to lie like a killing frost upon human relations" [1]

We can only wonder whether Einstein may have written this because he was aware that perhaps his own human relations may have been stunted by his competitiveness in the field of science.

The attitude of over-thinking or of being over-intellectual is a way of looking at things which is probably acquired through conditioning as much as it is genetically inherited. A purely intellectual attitude can come to us through our genes, our up-bringing and our formal education.

The main point Einstein seems to be making is that education places too much emphasis on learning facts and figures and fails to teach morality outside of a religious context. Einstein also repeatedly stressed the importance of the imagination over knowledge.

A further consideration is that morality and moral conduct cannot be properly imparted by "teaching" in the sense of yet more stifling factual instruction. The rationale behind all curricular and extracurricular activity should be to foster moral conduct as well as spiritual and intellectual growth.

One consequence of the emphasis on learning facts and figures is that "successful people" who go on to form an elite are the ones who score the highest in exams. They may be strong in facts and figures. But this has not usually been balanced by the development of other important qualities, for instance, consideration of the feelings of others. Many of these "successful" individuals are emotionally or morally unbalanced and can become difficult and destructive because they believe they are always right.

They lead their lives according to the Darwinian principle of 'Survival of the fittest.' These individuals have been taught competition leads to success and they believe in 'Survival of the brightest.'

When 'survival of those who are always right' becomes the norm it can lead to an elite class of emotionally and morally bankrupt individuals. Their greed for money, power and ego expansion goes hand in hand with plundering the planet.

There are many downsides to being over-intellectual. Perhaps one of the most damaging is believing or seeming to be fulfilled, when we are not.

This commonly happens because when we are right, we also 'think' we are happy, whereas being happy is not just a turn of phrase that goes with a superficial smile.

In turning situations into ones where being right triumphs over being happy our natural happiness is stifled with the result that we feel suffocated and repressed and we behave in restrained ways.

The damage that being purely intellectual has done to humanity may be partly reflected in the popularity and the vast amount of self-help books available in every developed country. Perhaps these self-help books could also denote a problem of success when success is defined in terms of being materially well off. Perhaps after having read them, self-help books become for the reader a badge of discontent. Maybe they support society's wish to make us believe we can be happy when we are not.

The acquisition of moral values is a vital part of education. It does not matter whether they are acquired at home, in school, in the jungle or in the city. Their acquisition cannot take place solely within the confines of a school or the home. These values also have to be acquired, tried and tested in the wider world.

Learning moral values is learning through observation, experience and relating to others. Moral values may also be acquired by example, instruction and training and also from reading.

Moral education is not just about learning what is right or wrong. Moral education is learning the 'ethos,' the characteristic spirit, culture, attitudes and aspirations of the community we live in, as well as of other communities in the wider world.

Einstein is also saying that the intellect has become too dominant in human interaction and is stifling and destroying mutual respect, trust and support.

Mutual aid, like mutual relating, involves people with similar experiences co-operating and helping each other to overcome difficulties. This involves a feeling of empathy between people.

Mutual aid was first outlined by Peter Kropotkin in his 1902 book entitled *Mutual Aid*, where he argues that avoidance of competition in the animal kingdom greatly increases the chances of survival and the quality of life. [2]

He formed these conclusions from his observations in Siberia of altruism in animals, insects and birds. He found that they frequently co-operated with each other in times of extremes of climatic conditions, when hunting and in times of danger.

Kropotkin's theory of co-operation is thought to be important for survival. His theory has been seen as a counterweight to Darwin's theory of 'survival of the fittest.' [3]

Mutual aid, as described by Kropotkin, can be observed in packs of dogs, shoals of fish, and flocks of birds. Additionally, multiple families of crows can be seen in our own gardens and backyards.

Recently, mutual aid groups sprang up spontaneously during the Pandemic of 2020 when people in communities helped one another cope by supplying food, medicines, fuel and collaborating with institutional support systems. Mutual aid is also practiced in all twelve step recovery groups for various addictions.

That Einstein was concerned with co-operation rather than confrontation is evident in his writing and his activism in the early peace movements of his time. As a result of his direct experience of German anti-Semitism, which forced him into exile, Einstein became even more deeply concerned with empathy, co-operation and mutual aid.

He saw the purely intellectual attitude as being unemotional and cold. He also felt that it was responsible for damaging and even destroying human relationships.

15.

Limitations of the Intellect, Psychology and Analysis

If we strive to understand ourselves, the world and the wider universe, we naturally and perhaps inevitably reach a point where we realise that our power to think is limited. For most of us it is a humbling experience to discover that we have reached the frontiers of our understanding and can go no further.

Perhaps the best we can do is accept that there is a superior intelligence which at once leaves us awestruck and baffled. We may also be content and even grateful to be able to enjoy the fruits available to us within our borders.

This principle applies not only when looking in awe at the wider world and the universe but also when we are in the presence of other people who are gifted in ways which we are not.

Einstein and Sigmund Freud met once, in the new year holidays of 1927 when Freud was staying in Berlin.

On 2nd January 1927 immediately after meeting with Einstein, Freud wrote to a Hungarian Psychoanalyst friend S. Ferenczi saying:

"He is cheerful, assured and courteous, understands as much about psychology as I do about physics, so we had a very pleasant talk." [1]

Freud could easily have written this after a meeting with any specialist or tradesman. It is an intentionally banal and even derogatory account of the meeting. There is an absence of anything psychological or descriptive of Einstein's personality and almost nothing about his thinking. Yet Freud was writing about a Nobel prize winner who had revolutionised the world of science!

Freud seems to be saying that he and Einstein had nothing much to say to each other on this occasion. It might also be worth pointing out that this is all the more astonishing because both of them played a major part in breaking loose from the shackles of the sedate world of the nineteenth century, opening up new vistas in their respective fields. Perhaps Freud was unwilling to put too much in writing at this stage, even to a friend, as private correspondence concerning celebrities is apt to become public when falling into the hands of the press.

Most significantly, Freud assumed that Einstein understood very little about psychology. On the contrary, as we shall see shortly, Einstein had been Carl Jung's guest at dinner several times in Zurich.

I think Freud may have been badly mistaken about Einstein's lack of understanding of 'basic' psychology of what motivates people and how and why they fiercely compete. I also think Freud was mistaken in thinking Einstein knew nothing of 'modern' psychology and particularly psychoanalysis, especially as Einstein had known Jung many years before meeting Freud.

There was clearly no love lost between these two great thinkers as Einstein showed shortly after the meeting. On 17 January 1927 Einstein replied to a request from H. Freund, a German psychotherapist friend, for him to take part in a study involving him undergoing psychoanalysis. It is not known if a reply was actually sent but on Freund's letter Einstein noted:

"I regret that I cannot accede to your request, because I should like very much to remain in the darkness of not having been analysed." [2]

In the October 1929 interview by G.G.Viereck of the Saturday Evening Post, Einstein gave what is probably one of the most

53

interesting and incisive opinions on the value of psychoanalysis.

"Then you do not believe in psychoanalysis?"

"I am not," Einstein modestly replied, "able to venture a judgment on so important a phase of modern thought. However, it seems to me that psychoanalysis is not always salutary. It may not always be helpful to delve into the subconscious.

"The machinery of our legs is controlled by a hundred different muscles. Do you think it would help us to walk, if we analysed our legs and knew exactly which one of the little muscles must be employed in locomotion and the order in which they work?

"Perhaps," he added with the whimsical smile that sometimes lights up the sombre pools of his eyes like a will-o'-the wisp, "you remember the story of the toad and the centipede? The centipede was very proud of having one hundred legs. His neighbour, the toad, was very much depressed because he had only four. One day a diabolic inspiration prompted the toad to write a letter to the centipede as follows:

'Honoured Sir: Can you tell me, which one of your hundred legs you move first when you transfer your distinguished body from one place to another and in what order you move the other ninety-nine legs?'
"When the centipede received this letter, he began to think. He tried first one leg, then the other. Finally, he discovered to his consternation that he was unable to move a single leg. He could no longer walk at all. He was paralysed! It is possible that analysis may paralyse our mental and emotional processes in a similar manner." [3] [4]

On December 6, 1931 Einstein made an interesting diary entry about the Swiss Psychiatrist Carl Jung:

"I understand Jung's vague, imprecise notions, but I consider them worthless; a lot of talk without any clear direction. If there has to be a psychiatrist, I should prefer Freud. I do not believe in him, but I love very much his concise style and his original, although rather extravagant mind." [5]

Einstein's understanding of both Freud and Jung are views many if not most medical doctors, psychiatrists, psychologists and psychotherapists still agree with. Jung's writing has always been considered 'woolly' whilst psychoanalysis is regarded as generally having no authority.

Whilst there is no doubt they integrated many ancient ideas and contributed many important new ideas to the new subject of psychology, Freud's and Jung's major works have never become mainstream in medicine, psychology, psychiatry or psychotherapy.

Psychoanalysis is an intellectual psychological exercise which is intended primarily as an analytical process and not necessarily a therapeutic process, as many distressed individuals eventually find out.

Anthony Storr, a respected English psychiatrist, interviewed Jung on 14th April 1951. Storr thought Jung suffered from psychotic symptoms and was convinced that Jung saw himself as a prophetic guru. These flaws are examined in *Feet of Clay - A Study of Gurus.* [6] [7]

There is no doubt that Jung suffered from a psychotic illness, as he himself admitted, nor is there any doubt that he saw himself as a prophetic guru. I doubt if his ideas came directly from his psychotic illness but his experience of illness enabled him to understand mental health problems in a way no others had done before him.

Jung's ideas, influenced by others before him, differ greatly from Freud. Freud focused on thinking, while Jung emphasised inner awareness and self-discovery. We will explore this concept of the Self with Ramana Maharshi.

16.

Path of the Choiceless

In 1931 Einstein was asked by the Institute for Intellectual Cooperation (a precursor to UNESCO - United Nations Educational, Scientific and Cultural Organization) to invite a thinker of his choosing to a cross-disciplinary exchange of ideas about politics and peace.

Einstein chose Freud, whom he had met briefly in 1927. On 30 July 1932 he invited Freud to be his correspondent. Their correspondence was published by the League of Nations on September 23rd 1933 as *"Why War?"* [1]

In his 1932 letter in "Why War?" Einstein asked Freud if he could help to answer how mankind can be saved from the menace of war threatening the very existence of civilisation. Einstein clarifies the question by describing what he sees as the underlying psychological causes of war. He attributes the causes of war to man's craving for power and money, as well as a lust for hatred and destructiveness, which he believes can escalate into a " "collective psychosis."

The idea of collective mental states was not a new concept but a "collective psychosis" was new. Einstein was the first person on record to use the term "collective psychosis." Coming up with a new psychological diagnostic term is hardly a feature of someone 'who knows little about psychology' as we saw earlier when Freud described Einstein after meeting him.

Freud's reply to Einstein's letter began by pointing out that in being asked to set out the problem of avoiding war from the position of a psychological observer, Einstein had taken the wind out of his sails. Freud's apparent irritation may have been from feeling not only eclipsed by Einstein but also feeling that

Einstein outshone him in his own field of psychology. Freud would have been aware that their written exchange was going to be printed and made public.

What seems particularly clear from Einstein's letter to Freud and Freud's reply is that Einstein had a deep understanding of the practical implications of the nature of psychology.

This is not what we would expect from Einstein, especially after Freud's remarks about him following their meeting in 1927. As we have already seen Freud said:

"He is cheerful, assured and courteous, understands as much about psychology as I do about physics, so we had a very pleasant talk."

Without venturing too far into psychology, this could just be a reflection of Freud's rather bitter personality. However it was most likely a defensive reaction, particularly in the presence of someone with such superior intelligence and is usually understood as an unconscious projection.

It is quite likely that Einstein heard about Freud's comment and in his humility, perhaps took it as harmlessly meant or even as a compliment.

On September 8th 1932 Freud wrote a belittling letter trivialising his "Why War?" correspondence with Einstein to Max Eitingon, a German psychoanalyst. There was no hint of gratitude for being invited to contribute to an interdisciplinary discussion of ideas about politics, peace and psychology.

"I have finished writing the tedious and sterile so-called discussion with Einstein."

But this was not to be the end of their correspondence. In May 1936 Freud replied to Einstein's letter which had congratulated him on his eightieth birthday:

"Of course I always knew that you admired me only 'out of politeness,' and that you are convinced of very few of my assertions . . . I hope that by the time you have reached my age you will have become a disciple of mine." [2]

This seems to be an example of Freud's arrogant paternalistic sense of humour. In spite of them having much in common, there is clearly an abyss between Einstein and Freud.

On January 30th 1933, Hitler became Chancellor of Germany. A few weeks later in March 1933, Einstein who was on a lecture tour of the United States, criticised Hitlers' repressive government.

On March 28th 1933, Einstein moved to Belgium where he handed in his German passport to the German Consulate in Brussels and renounced his German citizenship. Subsequently, Einstein's scientific works were publicly burned in Berlin and he was accused of spreading Communist propaganda. One German publication published a photograph of Einstein with the caption, 'not yet hanged.'

This prompted his wife Elsa Einstein to insist on not returning to Germany. After a great deal of persuasion from Elsa they left Belgium and arrived in Britain.

In June 1933 Einstein gave the Herbert Spencer lecture at Oxford and in July he went into hiding and stayed near the Norfolk town of Cromer on the estate of British MP Oliver Locker-Lampson for six weeks.

On 30th August 1933, Theodor Lessing, a German-Jewish philosopher associate of Einstein's, who also had a photograph with the caption, 'not yet hanged' was assassinated by the Nazis.

Just a few weeks later on Sept 23rd 1933, Einstein and Freud's

59

correspondence was published by the League of Nations as *Why War?*

On October 3rd Einstein gave a speech at the Royal Albert Hall in London and on October 7th he left London for the United States.

Eventually, on June 4th 1938, Freud and his family also left Austria and went into exile in Britain. Maybe with hindsight he re-appraised his discussion with Einstein as not having been so trivial and sterile after all. Perhaps Freud was secretly a little envious of Einstein's insights into why people go to war.

17.

Einstein's Impact on Psychology

Although we cannot be sure of Einstein's influence on Freud, he certainly had a profound influence on Jung. Einstein inspired Jung to come up with his theory of Synchronicity. In February 1953 Jung wrote with great respect about Einstein's genius as a thinker. In a letter to his confidant and personal doctor, Dr Seelig, Jung says:

25 February 1953

Dear Dr. Seelig,

I got to know Albert Einstein through one of his pupils, a Dr. Hopf, if I remember correctly.

Professor Einstein was my guest on several occasions at dinner, when, as you have heard, Adolf Keller was present on one of them and on others Professor Eugen Bleuler, a psychiatrist and my former chief.

These were very early days when Einstein was developing his first theory of relativity.

He tried to instil into us the elements of it, more or less successfully.

As non-mathematicians we psychiatrists had difficulty in following his argument.

Even so, I understood enough to form a powerful impression of him.

It was above all the simplicity and directness of his genius as a thinker that impressed me mightily and exerted a lasting influence on my own intellectual work.

It was Einstein who first started me off thinking about a possible relativity of time as well as space, and their psychic conditionality.

More than thirty years later this stimulus led to my relation with the physicist Professor W. Pauli and to my thesis of psychic synchronicity.

With Einstein's departure from Zurich my relation with him ceased, and I hardly think he has any recollection of me.

One can scarcely imagine a greater contrast than that between the mathematical and the psychological mentality.

The one is extremely quantitative and the other just as extremely qualitative.

With kind regards,

Yours sincerely,

C.G. Jung [1]

It is very likely that Einstein had a much greater impact than we are aware on how Freud's and Jung's thoughts influenced the emerging field of psychology and those who came after them.

In terms of understanding humankind and our predicaments, it is important to see how Einstein's conceptual thinking has influenced us. He showed that we can simply bend things, sometimes even back on themselves to understand them.

Einstein told us of the awe and veneration he experienced when contemplating the force behind the order and laws of nature. He admitted that there are forces we cannot understand, yet whose existence we must accept.

Modern psychology began with Freud's model of logical Analysis but this could not explain everything. Along came Jung, who from his own experiences showed other ways to examine ourselves. Although both Freud and Jung had their limitations they, like Einstein, enabled us to see ourselves from fresh perspectives.

We are now at a place where transpersonal psychology is encouraging us to turn back in on ourselves and look inside for answers which we had previously been taught and believed were outside us.

Transpersonal psychology is an umbrella term for a branch of psychology which includes looking at transcendent experiences as well as awareness of the human spirit.

It involves looking inside ourselves to seek our own truth, reality, morality and our own understanding of the unfathomable force behind nature, which may or may not be perceived as a Deity.

This takes us away from the purely rational thinking back to more conceptual thinking about reality, morality, God and religion, just as Einstein demonstrated by his use of thought experiments.

To understand where we are going, it helps to know where we have been and how we got here.

To grasp this psychological part of the journey of our understanding, we need to know about the four waves of psychology on which Transpersonal psychology is based.

The First wave

The First wave was 'psychoanalysis' initially developed by Sigmund Freud, who has been largely discredited [2] and later by Carl Jung who formulated much of his theory whilst suffering from a psychotic illness that lasted years. [3]

The Second wave

The Second wave of psychologists were 'behaviourists.' They tried to understand us only by our behaviour which we learn through conditioned interaction with the environment. It is limited because it does not include the appreciation of cognitive processes. In trying to understand ourselves only by our behaviour, behaviourists exclude the very essence of how we see ourselves to be what we are.

The Third wave

The Third wave of 'Humanistic Psychology' was the response largely by Carl Rogers and Abraham Maslow to the limitations of Psychoanalysis and Behavioural Psychology. This was based on man's drive to self-actualisation, the process of realising our own capabilities.

The Fourth wave

The Fourth wave, 'Transpersonal Psychology,' includes and complements the first three and is based on the need to include the spiritual in all its many forms. It is largely due to Roberto Assagioli's work in Psychosynthesis and Abraham Maslow's work, together with the earlier work of Carl Jung and Viktor Frankl in his book *Man's Search for Meaning*. [4]

This movement sprang up in 1969 and was not surprisingly just after the summer of love in 1967 with its challenge to traditional authority. My psychotherapy teachers, Ian Gordon-Brown and Barbara Somers, were the leading teachers of Transpersonal Psychology in the UK and gave an account of its main precepts in *'The Raincloud of Unknowable things.'* [5]

An important influence in that direction was from the Beatles' promotion of mantra meditation in 1967. George Harrison played a particularly sincere and important role in this.

Transpersonal psychology integrates modern psychology with the ancient wisdom of Vedanta, Judaism, Buddhism, Christian Mysticism, Sufism, meditation, alchemy and various forms of divination, including the concept of synchronicity. [6]

Synchronicity is the term used by Jung for the coincidence of two events.

The initial idea of synchronicity was inspired by one of Einstein's discussions with Jung over dinner regarding relativity.

However, as Jung said, it was only many years later, with the help of the physicist Wolfgang Pauli, that Einstein was able to develop the concept. [7]

It could be seen as a mere coincidence that eventually Transpersonal psychology emerged as the most developed and meaningful forms of psychology integrating modern psychology with the ancient wisdom of Vedanta, Judaism, Buddhism, Christian Mysticism, Sufism meditation, alchemy and various forms of divination including synchronicity.

Or could it be that Einstein's warning and advice given below, was heeded by Jung and others?

Let us revisit what Einstein said in 1937 and review how psychology got to where it is today. As we have already seen, these were traditions Einstein warned man not to forget when he advised:

"Our time is distinguished by wonderful achievements in the fields of scientific understanding and technical application of those insights. Who would not be cheered by this? But let us not forget that knowledge and skills alone cannot lead humanity to a happy and dignified life. Humanity has every reason to place the proclaimers of high moral standards and values above the discoveries of objective truth. What humanity owes to personalities like Buddha, Moses, and Jesus ranks for me higher than all the achievements of the enquiring and constructive mind.

What these blessed men have given us we must guard and try to keep alive with all our strength if humanity is not to lose its dignity, the security of its existence, and joy in living." [8]

This is profound advice and also a warning not to forget our moral standards and values. Einstein emphasises that above everything else, morality is the most important thing for us to lead a happy, dignified and secure life.

Einstein is reminding us of the high moral standards and values which the original pioneers of religions showed us. He is not talking about the religious leaders of his time whom he knew had lost their way. He was talking particularly about high moral standards and values from the East.

Several years later in 1944, Jung wrote a long introduction to Heinrich Zimmer's book on Ramana Maharshi, *The Way to the Self*, which echoed Einstein's advice and warning.

"Obviously the outward lives of men could do with a lot more bettering and beautifying, but these things lose their meaning when the inner man does not keep pace with them. To be satiated with "necessities" is no doubt an inestimable source of happiness, yet the inner man continues to raise his claim, and this can be satisfied by no outward possessions. And the less this voice is heard in the chase after the brilliant things of this world, the more the inner man becomes the source of inexplicable misfortune and uncomprehended unhappiness in the midst of living conditions whose outcome was expected to be entirely different.

The externalization of life turns to incurable suffering, because no one can understand why he should suffer from himself. No one wonders at his insatiability, but regards it as his lawful right, never thinking that the one-sidedness of this psychic diet leads in the end to the gravest disturbances of equilibrium." [9]

18.

Losing Our Way then Remembering Einstein

Method without Meaning

In the 20th Century, many spiritual teachers from the East introduced meditation techniques to the West. One of these techniques, in the early 1900's was Ramana Maharshi's 'Self-enquiry'. Another, in the 1960s, was Thich Nhat Hanh's 'Mindfulness.'

Some of the techniques from their teachings like 'mantra meditation' and 'mindfulness' were hoisted from their broader context by commercially minded individuals.

They were westernised with claims they had 'scientifically' measurable health benefits, which were regarded as highly questionable. Their promotion and marketing transformed the selling of these into lucrative businesses.

The selling of these techniques undoubtedly showed many individuals that there was a level of consciousness which they had not previously been aware of, which for most, was of course, was a good thing. Even more important, these techniques also made other individuals aware that there was much more behind what they had been taught and had not been told about.

The origins of these techniques hijacked from Hinduism and Buddhism had greater meaning and depth than were revealed by those who marketed and sold them. The spiritual and religious terminology they arrived with in the West, like any mention of God, had been quickly dropped to improve public relations and increase sales. [1]

These meditation techniques were never meant to be standalone techniques for the sole purpose of disengaging from thinking as a method of relaxation and stress relief.

These techniques from the East were originally developed as only a part of the way to begin to concentrate on turning inside to access deeper levels of understanding ourselves and the universe. When these hijacked techniques were sold to the West they were not used with this original intention in mind.

What happened was that some of the tools of Ramana Maharshi and Thich Nhat Hanh were cherry picked, separated from their teachings and taught as standalone relaxation and stress reduction tools.

Individuals were being taught methods without their true meaning. We will examine this in greater depth when we look at 'Understanding Method and Truth.'

It is no surprise that many of the most serious original teachers of mindfulness and mantra meditation eventually stopped promoting them as they had the insight to see there were higher levels of awareness which they could attain. Many of these teachers went to the earlier pioneers to find their original deeper meaning. Very often this was to follow the teachings of either Ramana Maharshi or Thich Nhat Hanh.

It seems that somehow, Einstein's message was listened to about guarding what we have been given by the likes of Buddha, Moses and Jesus when he wrote:

"What these blessed men have given us we must guard and try to keep alive with all our strength if humanity is not to lose its dignity, the security of its existence, and joy in living." [2]

69

19.

The Bliss of No Want

In the October 1929 interview by G.G.Viereck of the Saturday Evening Post, Einstein spoke about the relationship between happiness and having no desires.

"I am happy because I want nothing from anyone. I do not care for money. Decorations, titles or distinctions mean nothing to me. I do not crave praise. The only thing that gives me pleasure apart from my work, my violin and my boat, is the appreciation of my fellow workers." [1] [2]

Ramana Maharshi frequently stated that the desire of everyone is happiness. He also said that it was not to be found in any external objects but inside.

'No want' is the greatest bliss. It can be realised only by experience. Even an emperor is no match for a man with no want. [3]

When they say they have no wants, both Einstein and Ramana Maharshi only want to be left to fulfil what they see as their life's purpose.

Einstein spoke about the emptiness of outward success, of acquiring material possessions, of gaining public attention and luxury.

"Without the sense of collaborating with like-minded beings in the pursuit of the ever unattainable in art and scientific research, my life would have been empty. Ever since childhood I have scorned the commonplace limits so often set upon human ambition. Possessions, outward success, publicity, luxury – to me these have always been contemptible. I believe that a simple and unassuming manner of life is best for everyone, best both for the body and the mind." [4]

For Einstein, comradeship, scientific research and music were lifelong interests and helped give meaning to his life. He did not crave money, power, fame or luxuries. Einstein led a simple life and sometimes spoke as if he were a stoic.

As already mentioned, one of Einstein's main pleasures was sailing. Such was Einstein's disregard for death that although he never learnt to swim, he refused to carry lifejackets on his sailing-boat.

As we saw earlier, soon after Hitler became Chancellor of Germany photographs of Einstein appeared with the caption, *'not yet hanged'*. Einstein seemed unconcerned about the danger.

It was his wife, Elsa Einstein, who insisted that they emigrate. Apparently after a great deal of persuasion from Elsa they left continental Europe and arrived in Britain in early September 1933.

Ramana Maharshi also had a similar attitude of disregard to the threat of danger and death. The following account was given by a retired lawyer B.V. Narasimha Swami:

'At 11.30 pm on June 26th 1924, thieves broke into the Ashram and smashed the glass panes of a window. They then mercilessly beat Ramana Maharshi who sat calmly. They also beat his attendants. He said, 'Let them play their role; we shall stick to ours. Let them do what they like. It is for us to bear and forebear. Let us not interfere with them.' eventually the thieves left.' [5]

These two remarkable men shared an almost nonchalant attitude concerning precautions against danger and death. We can only

71

assume they believed so utterly their lives were predetermined that it caused them little or no anxiety.

20.

Proving what Science Denies

In 1936 a child from New York wrote to Einstein asking him if scientists pray and if so, what they pray for. He gave the child a detailed and articulate reply.

"Scientific research is based on the idea that everything that takes place is determined by laws of nature, and therefore this holds for the actions of people. For this reason, a research scientist will hardly be inclined to believe that events could be influenced by a prayer, i.e. by a wish addressed to a supernatural Being.

However, it must be admitted that our actual knowledge of these laws is only imperfect and fragmentary, so that, actually, the belief in the existence of basic all-embracing laws in nature also rests on a sort of faith. All the same this faith has largely been justified so far by the success of scientific research. But on the other hand, everyone who is seriously involved in the pursuit of science becomes convinced that a spirit is manifest in the laws of the Universe-a spirit vastly superior to that of man, and one in the face of which we with our modest powers must feel humble. In this way the pursuit of science leads to a religious feeling of a special sort, which is indeed quite different from the religiosity of someone more naïve." [1]

Einstein's reply to the child is a masterpiece of care, tact and humility.

He says research scientists see everything that takes place is determined by the laws of nature [not by wishful prayers].

Einstein seems to be saying that scientific researchers initially tend to be agnostic but eventually everyone who studies the laws of nature seriously nonetheless becomes convinced of a spirit vastly superior to that of man which is manifest in the laws of the Universe.

Whilst Einstein reasons that there must be a superior spirit behind the laws of the universe, he falls short of being explicit and admitting that he himself also believes what all other research scientists eventually come to believe.

Perhaps he thought he did not need to say this because he assumed it goes without saying that he too believes what all other research scientists believe. This is my understanding of Einstein's own religious feeling.

He also points out that scientific thinking leads to a religious feeling different to those who are more naïve [those who follow organised religions].

Because our intelligence is limited by words and thoughts, we cannot appreciate the existence of a vastly superior spirit by thinking further about it than we are capable of. We can only appreciate this further by our 'awareness 'of it.

Einstein uses his reasoning to explain why he doesn't believe in God as a personal God such as in organised religions. However, he is convinced of a spirit as the force behind the order and laws in nature. He uses a combination of intuition and scientific rational thinking as a different framework for the existence of a cosmic God that is not unlike the Brahman of Ramana Maharshi.

This spirit is his own term for a non-personal God. This is simply looking at most people's 'God' from a different viewing point and calling it a 'spirit vastly superior to man.' It is the same God, just named differently to express how he has arrived at his conviction. Einstein's euphemism for God is spirit.

Einstein had a sceptic's curiosity which was transformed into awe by realising the unfathomable vastly superior intelligent force behind nature's laws.

Einstein went to considerable lengths to explain his notion of what God is and what God is not. In our attempt to understand his religious experience we can compare and contrast our own understanding and experiences to review our own ideas on what we regard as God. We might even change our long-held beliefs one way or another.

If several people stand around an unknown object looking at it from different angles, they each have a different view. Each person might see it differently and even call it something else, but, in its entirety, it is still the same thing. Whether they call the unknown object nature's lawmaker, God, Supernatural, the Force, or the Spirit, it is still the same Entity.

A parable, possibly from the Hindu Rigveda, is thought to have been written down from earlier oral traditions. It therefore dates back to between 1500 and 1200 BCE. It is usually known as 'The Blind Men and the Elephant'. It also appears in Buddhist, Sufi and Jain texts and is the basis of Idries Shah's book The Elephant in the Dark. [2] The story has several variations, but broadly goes as follows:

A group of blind men heard that a strange animal, called an elephant, had been brought to the town, but none of them were aware of its shape and form. Out of curiosity, they said:

"We must inspect and know it by touch, of which we are capable." So, they sought it out, and when they found it they felt it with their hands.

The first person, whose hand landed on the trunk, said: "This elephant is like a thick snake."

The second man whose hand reached its ear said: "It seems like a kind of fan."

The third person, whose hand was upon its leg, said: "This elephant is a pillar like a tree-trunk."

The blind man who placed his hand upon its side said: "The elephant is a wall".

The fifth man who felt its tail said: "It is as a rope."

The last man felt its tusk, which was smooth and pointed, and concluded that the elephant was a spear.

Their definitions of the elephant are clearly different from each other. In some versions, the blind men even accuse each other of being dishonest and they come to blows. The moral of the parable is that humans have a tendency to claim absolute truth based on their limited, subjective experience. But they reject the perspectives of other people which may be equally valid.[3]

Idries Shah's 'Commentary on the allegory is interesting:

"According to their conditioning they produce the answer. Now look at their answers. Some will say that this is a fascinating and touching allegory of the presence of God. Others will say that it is showing people how stupid mankind can be. Some say it is anti-scholastic. Others that it is just a tale copied by Rumi from Sanai – and so on" [4]

The Rigveda, sums it up:

"Reality is one, though wise men speak of it variously."

21.

Einstein and Brahman.

In 1930, when the Indian poet, philosopher, musician and Nobel prize winner, Rabindranath Tagore met with Einstein in Germany, Einstein was already aware of Brahman, the Hindu conception of a cosmic God. The discussion between the two Nobel Prize winners was recorded on July 14, 1930. In speaking about Brahman Tagore said:

The most likely reason for the meeting between Einstein and Tagore was that they were both Nobel Prize winners and so were thought to be compatible and possibly an interesting combination. But the meeting did not bring about the cross-fertilisation of minds that had been hoped for.

"According to the Indian philosophy there is Brahman, the absolute truth, which cannot be conceived by the isolation of the individual mind or described by words but can be realized only by merging the individual in its infinity. But such a truth cannot belong to science. The nature of truth which we are discussing is an appearance; that is to say, what appears to be true to the human mind, and therefore is human, and may be called maya, or illusion." [1]

Einstein did not agree with Tagore about truth. Perhaps this was because Tagore's use of the word truth could easily have been substituted with the word reality and this may have caused misunderstanding. As we will see in the chapter on truth, truth varies from person to person.

Ramana Maharshi did not believe in a personal God. His experience of God is more aligned with Brahman, the concept of God in the Vedanta Hindu philosophy. Brahman is understood as the ultimate universal reality, the cause of everything that exists, uniting everything, including consciousness, as a single binding unity.

From the transcript of the recording of the meeting between the two Nobel Prize winners, the meeting did not go swimmingly. There was minimal agreement, limited discussion, and no common ground between their polarised religious, philosophical, and scientific perspectives.

Could it be that Tagore was prejudiced against science? Perhaps the gulf between the two Nobel prize winners was that for Einstein science was a source of "religious awe" whereas for Tagore the study of science belonged not to Brahman but to the realm of Maya. And never the twain shall meet.

The main point of disagreement was on the nature of reality. Tagore believed that reality exists because of man's consciousness of it, whilst Einstein believed that reality exists without man having to observe it and be aware of it. The most striking example of their opposing beliefs was when Einstein said that Tagore would not accept that a table in the house they were in would exist if nobody was in the house.

Without going too deeply into philosophy, Einstein believed in the existence of objects 'in themselves,' separate from human existence, that is, in a reality unknowable to us. This is consciousness independent reality. [2]

The opposite of this is the belief in objects as they appear and are known only to our consciousness through our sensory apparatus. The sensory apparatus in our brain also needs our intuition of space and time to create our reality. This is consciousness dependent reality, which was Tagore's belief. [3]

Tagore believed in the reality of objects which our consciousness has a part in creating with our sensory apparatus. Whereas Einstein believed in objects in themselves as separate from human consciousness.

As we will see shortly, Ramana Maharshi gave a different and more encompassing explanation of reality. I mention this because one of the world's other great physicists, and formerly Einstein's mentor, Max Planck, had a different understanding. He believed that everything is dependent on consciousness.

In the January 1931 interview with 'The Observer' Max Planck, now a friend of Einstein's and fellow Nobel prize winner, made a statement that was highly remarkable.

'I regard consciousness as fundamental. I regard matter as derivative from consciousness. We cannot get behind consciousness. Everything that we talk about, everything that we regard as existing, postulates consciousness.' [4]

This was an exceptionally insightful and profound statement from one of the world's most respected physicists. His idea resonates with the belief known as panpsychism which asserts that consciousness is the fundamental feature of reality throughout the universe.

The idea of panpsychism is not new. It is one of the oldest philosophical theories and was attributed first to the Ancient Greek pre-Socratic philosopher, Thales, who lived from 626-548 BCE. It also formed part of the thinking of Plato, Spinoza, Leibniz, Schopenhauer, William James and Bertrand Russell.

Panpsychism has enjoyed a revived interest in the 21st century in the fields of neuroscience, psychology, and quantum mechanics. It directly addresses the problem of consciousness. [5]

It remains to be seen what the scientific study of consciousness will reveal to mankind. But at the present time panpsychism does seem to be a step in a new direction, especially for scientists.
It is possible that scientists will eventually conclude that

Consciousness cannot be fully understood by the thinking mind. This would certainly be the case if they came to accept that thinking is in fact derived from Consciousness. This line of thought chimes with Ramana Maharshi's surrender and subordination of thoughts to Awareness.

If it is eventually shown and accepted that everything comes from consciousness, then we would be wise to turn and look at the Indian Vedantic tradition that everything in the world of the senses is an illusion (maya). We would also do well to look at the significance of the dreamtime of the Australians Aboriginals as well as the importance of consciousness in other cultures.

Australian Aboriginals are deeply introverted and devoutly spiritual because their reality is not of this world but of another which cannot be seen. To Aborigines the Dreamtime includes living by the belief that each person's spirit comes from the spirit of something from the Earth, like an animal, a bird, a tree, or a particular rock in a particular place. When a rock person dies, they return there to the soil to be reborn. Hence it is very important to Aborigines to look after their land, which they intimately identify with as being their own spirit. [6]

I have mentioned Max Planck's belief in panpsychism to demonstrate a leading physicist's understanding of reality which is different from Einstein's and Tagore's. They each have contrasting viewpoints that may be encompassed and reconciled by the broader perspective of Ramana Maharshi.

Einstein and Ramana Maharshi never met, and it would have been most unlikely for their paths ever to cross. Einstein travelled widely and moved in international circles of science, politics, the arts, peace activism, and entertainment. Ramana Maharshi did not travel and only became well known later in his life after the 1934 publication of Paul Brunton's *A Search in Secret India.* [7]

On 24th January, 1938 Ramana Maharshi was asked about

illusion.

Q: Are there degrees of illusion?

M: Illusion is itself illusory. Illusion must be seen by one beyond it. Can such a seer be subject to illusion? Can he then speak of degrees of illusion? There are scenes floating on the screen in a cinema show. Fire appears to burn buildings to ashes. Water seems to wreck vessels. But the screen on which the pictures are projected remains unscorched and dry. Why? Because the pictures are unreal and the screen is real. Again reflections pass through a mirror; but the mirror is not in any way affected by the quality or quantity of the reflections on it. So the world is a phenomenon on the single reality, which is not affected in any manner. Reality is only one. The discussion about illusion is due to the difference in the angle of vision. Change your angle of vision to one of jnana [knowledge of the Self] and then find the universe to be only Brahman. Being now in the world, you see the world as such. Get beyond it and this will disappear: the reality alone will shine. [8]

Before we examine the teachings of Ramana Maharshi in greater detail it would be worth looking at how truth may vary from one person to another.

22.

Truth

Einstein and Ramana Maharshi had a different conception of God. Much of Einstein's life was concerned with trying to understand the force behind the order and laws of nature by conceptual thinking, logic and mathematics using the empirical universe as his laboratory. Ramana Maharshi's life was concerned with turning inwards and experiencing awareness of being one with everything.

Something you see from your position with your eyes is your perspective only. It is what you perceive with your senses which informs what you consider to be truth. That is one reason why we cannot easily say what truth is. Truth is our truth only, everyone else has their own truth too. We cannot know anyone else's truth, only ours. But sometimes we can step back to attempt to understand other points of view. There is an inspiring story of Nasrudin.

Nasrudin was a Mullah. He may have been from a number of countries: Afghanistan, Iran, Turkey, India... perhaps even Greece or Russia. Nobody knows for sure. For centuries stories of Nasrudin have been used to poke fun at authority. There are many stories about him. This is one about truth.

How Nasrudin created Truth

The King decided that he could, and would, make people observe the truth. He would make them practise truthfulness.

Mullah Nasrudin tactfully told the King that laws alone do not improve individuals. Behaviour should be aligned with deeper truth.

Entry to the King's city was by a bridge. On the bridge he built a gallows.

The following day, when the gates were opened at dawn, the Captain of the Guard was stationed with a squad of troops to question all who entered.

An announcement was made: "Everyone who wishes to enter the city must answer some questions. Those who tell the truth, will be allowed to enter. Anyone who lies, will be hanged." Nasrudin stepped forward.

"Where are you going?" asked one of the guards.
"I am on my way," said Nasrudin slowly, "to be hanged."
"We don't believe you!"
"Very well, if I have told a lie, hang me!"
"But if we hang you for lying, we will have made what you said come true! We don't want to prove you were telling the truth."
"Yes indeed," said the Mullah. Now you know what truth is - Your truth. It is deeper than you previously thought" [1]

Our individual perspective can be all important. One side of an object can be a different colour from its other side. People sit in different places, with different postures, different intentions, moods, problems, backgrounds, histories and different genetic and epigenetic influences.

Although we may be looking at the same thing, it appears different to each of us, but only because of our different standpoints. In reality, it is the same thing.

We may seem similar, but our perspectives can vary greatly. Those who tell you how happy they are and those who tell you all the things you need to be happy, are only speaking from their own perspective. They may be saying what they think you want or need to hear or they may be saying what they want to say, without considering you.

Einstein's chosen philosopher, Spinoza, put the moral of the Nasrudin story in a nutshell 350 years ago:

"Simplicity and truth of character are not produced by the constraint of laws, nor by the authority of the state, No one the whole world over can be forced or legislated into a state of blessedness." [2]

Nasrudin at the Bank

There is one more amusing story of Nasrudin which shines a light on the dilemma of how we understand truth and reality.

Nasrudin goes into a bank to withdraw some money. He walks up to the bank cashier and says,

"I want to withdraw some money."
The cashier looks at him and asks him, "Can you identify yourself?"
Nasrudin reaches into his jacket pocket and pulls out a mirror, holds it up to his face, looks at it and says, "It is me."

There are different kinds of 'truth.' The cashier wants some identification which matches the bank's criteria. This could be an ID card, a passport or a driving licence which the bank would accept as 'official' identification.
Nasrudin knows who he is on a deeper level than the artificial image of himself that would satisfy the cashier. When he says who he is, his truth is real, both personally and absolutely. When officials require proof of identity such as an identity card, passport or driving licence, they often fail to realise they are operating on such a superficial level. One irony is that the document they insist on could also be a fake.

PART TWO

Ramana Maharshi

23.

Essence of Awareness

In some respects it is difficult to imagine two more completely different people than Einstein and Ramana Maharshi. Einstein, a giant among scientists and intellectuals, developed the theory of relativity. He travelled the world lecturing, wrote over 300 scientific papers and over 150 non-scientific papers.

Ramana Maharshi lived on the lower slopes of a sacred hill for 56 years. He only spoke occasionally, preferring instead to remain silent in the inner stillness of Self-realisation. He did not travel and wrote little.

Ramana Maharshi was never famous like Einstein and was only well known in the last fifteen years of his life. However, he was described by Carl Jung as 'the whitest spot on a white surface' [1]

He was known for being a living example of a Self-realised man emanating a silent force of peace and stillness. Today he is still regarded as the most important 20th Century guru of consciousness.

His legacy is what he described as the 'direct' path, or final common path to which all attempts at realisation must eventually converge. The presence of the silent stillness he emanated, and the few words he spoke, helped followers of this path to experience awareness of this oneness for themselves by the shortest route.

The following is an attempt to explain this awareness. However, any explanation is limited because inner experience is difficult to convey in words. Certain things can only be known by being experienced. Absolute Truth has no words.

Ramana Maharshi's teaching is simple. It is this: who you believe you are, is not you. You consider your thoughts and your body to be you, whereas your bundles of thoughts and bodily sensations all derive from Awareness. You are this Awareness.

The mind has several vital functions. Thinking serves the body, keeping it safe, warm, fed, clothed, supporting it materially, and ensuring it behaves in ways so it can survive. The domain of thinking includes your personality, the intellect, emotions, memories and desires. The mind processes all the information arriving in the brain from the senses of sight, touch, hearing, taste and smell. It is the body's manager. These functions are about external concerns.

The ego manages external information and thoughts about external objects. Identifying with these thoughts (the ego) limits your understanding of your true self. Though generated by you, these thoughts are not you.

Your difficulty is that you have become stuck believing you are the bundles of thoughts (the ego) doing these things (the doer) instead of knowing you *are* the Awareness behind the thinker and the doer. You have become separated from your Awareness, your true inner Self. Living in the modern competitive world demands that you remain in the thinking mode most of the time. Thinking is obviously necessary for basic survival and day-to-day duties living and working with others. But this is not who you really are.

Identifying with our thoughts and bodily sensations is our delusion of separateness. It is an illusion that is generally corroborated by the people around us. We continue to accept that we are this 'thinking ego' until a crisis is triggered by great loss, change or suffering.

When you are unhappy, suffering or overwhelmed by pain or pressure, you may seek a new direction. After much searching for solutions in the external world, you may see that, paradoxically, the way out is in.

Ramana Maharshi's teaching centres on turning inwards and experiencing inner Awareness by being still and just being.

In order to avoid any inadvertent misrepresentation or distortion of Ramana Maharshi's teachings on Awareness, I will frequently quote his own words.

24.

Awakening

Miserable Mundane Life

Ramana Maharshi's awakening to what was to be his lifelong path was similar to Einstein's discovery of science and mathematics in that it took place at an early age. But the paths they then followed were strikingly different. Einstein had a powerful visual imagination and an extensive knowledge of the philosophers. He immersed himself in the external knowledge acquired from fellow physicists. He used mathematics as his main tool. Ramana Maharshi, by way of contrast, turned inside to be still and was immersed in Awareness.

Although Ramana Maharshi may be considered a unique phenomenon, many can relate to the difficulties he encountered in his childhood. His quest was fundamentally the same as our own.

When he was twelve years old his father died with the result that his family was broken up. He moved to Dindigul with his mother and then to Madurai to live with his uncle. At twelve years old he experienced the pain of losing his father, seeing his mother's grief, the upheaval of leaving his parental home, leaving his school and his friends as well as having to move in with an uncle. This was an abrupt end to a carefree childhood with his parents, siblings and friends. He tells of being rescued from the pain and misery of 'mundane' life in a poem '*The Necklet of nine Gems*' in the '*Collected Works*' when he writes:

'To rescue me - born of virtuous Sundara and Sundari in the holy place of Tiruchuli, seat of Bhuminatheswara - from the pain of miserable mundane life, He raised me to His state, that His heart might so rejoice, the immanence of Siva so shine forth, and the Self flourish. Such is Arunachala, famous throughout the universe!' [1]

His difficult adolescence opened a path in him towards Self-realisation. It provided an exit path away from what he described as 'the pain of miserable mundane life.'

The first experience occurred in November 1895 when a visiting elderly relative mentioned that he had just returned from a sacred hill, Arunachala. The young Venkantaraman (Ramana) had previously not known that the sacred Arunachala was a real place. It was the sacred hill, Arunachala that was the 'guru' who would rescue him.

The second experience occurred around this time when he read a book his uncle had given him about sixty-three Tamil saints, 'Peria Puranam,' which left a great impression on him.

Self-realisation

His third experience was a few months later in mid July 1896. It transformed him from being a boy to a sage. He spontaneously practiced Self-enquiry and permanently realised his Self with absolute certainty. He describes having this experience at 16 years old . . .

'I was sitting alone in a room on the first floor of my uncle's house. I seldom had any sickness, and on that day there was nothing wrong with my health, but a sudden violent fear of death overtook me. There was nothing in my state of health to account for it, and I did not try to account for it or to find out whether there was any reason for the fear. I just felt 'I am going to die' and began thinking what to do about it. It did not occur to me to consult a doctor, or my elders or friends; I felt that I had to solve the problem myself, there and then.

The shock of the fear of death drove my mind inwards and I said to myself mentally, without actually framing the words: 'Now death has come; what does it mean? What is it that is dying? The body dies.' And I at once dramatised the occurrence of death. I lay with my limbs stretched out stiff as though rigor mortis had set in, and imitated a corpse so as to give greater reality to the enquiry. I held my breath and kept my lips tightly closed so that no sound could escape, so that neither the word 'I' nor any other word could be uttered. 'Well then,' I said to myself, 'this body is dead. It will be carried stiff to the burning ground and there burnt and reduced to ashes. But with the death of this body am I dead? Is the body I? It is silent and inert but I feel the full force of my personality and even the voice of the "I" within me, apart from it. So I am Spirit transcending the body. The body dies but the Spirit that transcends it cannot be touched by death. That means I am the deathless Spirit.' All this was not dull thought; it flashed through me vividly as living truth which I perceived directly, almost without thought-process. 'I' was something very real, the only real thing about my present state, and all the conscious activity connected with my body was centred on that 'I'. From that moment onwards the 'I' or Self, focused attention on Itself by a powerful fascination. Fear of death had vanished once and for all. Absorption in the Self continued unbroken from that time on.' [2]

Thus from the age of sixteen, he was to remain permanently in the state of being fully realised. When he saw an opportunity of going to the hill, Arunachala, which he had not previously known actually existed, he simply left his uncle's home to live on Arunachala for good.

He left Madurai on August 29th 1896 and arrived in Arunachala on September 1st 1896.

Nearly fifty years later on 22nd November 1945, he was asked to recount this first experience.

'When I lay down with limbs outstretched and mentally

91

enacted the death scene and realised that the body would be taken and cremated and yet I would live, some force, call it atmic [Self or Soul] power or anything else, rose within me and took possession of me. With that, I was reborn and I became a new man. I became indifferent to everything afterwards, having neither likes nor dislikes." [3]

When Ramana Maharshi recalled his awakening as realising his body would be taken for cremation, yet knowing he would still live, he described experiencing an 'atmic' power which rose within him. He says he had mentally enacted the death scene which enabled this experience to occur.

There is a remarkable similarity between Ramana Maharshi's mentally enacting the death scene during his awakening, and Einstein's use of conceptual thinking in his imaginative thought experiments from where he was able to discover and describe his theory of relativity.

Ramana Maharshi's description of the rising of an 'atmic' power is important. Atmic come from the term Atman meaning the 'Self' which is completely identical (Advaita, Non-Dual) with the ultimate reality, Brahman.

They both used imaginative conceptual thinking to uncover hidden perspectives.

25.

Arunachala

The hill Arunachala became the young Venkataraman's (Ramana's) guru when he was nearly 16 years old in November 1895.

One day he overheard a visitor in his house talking, when the word Arunachala caught his ear. He enquired from this elderly relative, whom he had known in Tiruchuli, whence he had come: From Arunachala he was told. "What! From Arunachala?" the boy exclaimed, amazed that this was a place to which one could go. The relative, wondering in his turn at the ignorance of callow youth, explained that Arunachala was Tiruvannamalai. The sudden realization that the Holy Hill was a real, tangible place on earth that one could visit overwhelmed Venkataraman with awe and intense joy. [1]

Ramana Maharshi regarded the hill Arunachala not only as his guru but also as a manifestation of Brahman. He wrote several poems about Arunachala which include:

The Necklet of nine Gems

The Marital Garland of Letters

Five Hymns to Arunachala

Eleven Verses to Sri Arunachala

Eight Stanzas to Sri Arunachala

Five Stanzas to Sri Arunachala

These poems reveal his experience of Self-realisation. In the Marital Garland of Letters he mentions the destruction of the ego.

"Thou dost root out the ego of those who meditate on Thee in the heart, Oh Arunachala!" [2]

"I came to feed on Thee, but Thou hast fed on me; now there is peace, Oh Arunachala!" [3]

The poems are all like deeply devotional love poems as in:

Five Stanzas to Sri Arunachala

1. Ocean of nectar, full of grace, engulfing the universe in Thy splendour! Oh Arunachala, the Supreme itself! Be Thou the sun and open the lotus of my heart in Bliss!

2. Oh Arunachala! In Thee the picture of the universe is formed, has its stay, and is dissolved; this is the sublime truth. Thou art the inner Self, who dancest in the Heart as 'I'. 'Heart' is Thy name, Oh Lord!

3. He who turns inward with untroubled mind to search where the consciousness of 'I' arises, realizes the Self, and rests in Thee, Oh Arunachala! Like a river when it joins the ocean.

4. Abandoning the outer world, with mind and breath controlled, to meditate on Thee within, the yogi sees Thy light, Oh Arunachala! And finds his delight in Thee.

5. He who dedicates his mind to Thee and, seeing Thee, always beholds the universe as Thy figure, he who at all times glorifies Thee and loves Thee as none other than the Self, he is the master without rival, being one with Thee, Oh Arunachala, and lost in Thy bliss! [4]

Ramana Maharshi moved to live on and around the hill Arunachala after he became self-realised in 1896 aged 16. He lived in silence for the first 11 years, occasionally writing answers to visitors' questions. Then around 1907 he gradually resumed speech and lived in caves on Arunachala for over 20 years.

As we will see, Ramana Maharshi was silent most of his life, only speaking about once every five days. When he did speak, it was to pass his teaching on to those who did not understand his silent teaching, which he regarded as more direct. His silent teaching is still regarded as the best today.

Arunachala is part of the temple town of Tiruvannamalai. It soars 2669 feet, 800 meters high. The road around the Arunachala is 8 ½ miles (14 kms) and is known as the Giri Pradakshina Road. The 'Pradakshina' walk around Arunachala, includes the Arunachalam Temple which is at the base of Arunachala and takes three to four hours.

26.

Levels of Attainment

On 16th December 1938 Ramana Maharshi was questioned about different levels of experiencing of religion. His answers were similar in structure to Einstein's. He explained the levels experienced depend on the nature of the seeker. His answers need no explanation as they are direct and unambiguous.

Q. "Is the experience of the Highest State the same to all? Or is there any difference?"

M. The Highest State is the same and the experience is also the same.

Q. But I find some difference in the interpretations put on the Highest Truth.

M. The interpretations are made with the mind. The minds are different and so the interpretations are different.

Q. I mean to ask if the seers express themselves differently?

M. The expressions may differ according to the nature of the seekers. They are meant to guide the seekers. One seer speaks in the terms of Christianity, another in those of Islam, a third of Buddhism, etc. Is that due to their upbringing? Whatever may be their upbringing, their experience is the same. But the modes of expression differ according to circumstances. [1]

The next day Ramana Maharshi was asked to continue his answer from the previous day.

Q. Sri Bhagavan said last night that God is guiding us. Then why should we make an effort to do anything?

M. Who asks you to do so? If there was that faith in the guidance of God this question would not have arisen.

Q. The fact is that God guides us. Then what is the use of these instructions to people?

M. They are for those who seek instructions. If you are firm in your belief in the guidance of God, stick to it, and do not concern yourself with what happens around you. Furthermore, there may be happiness or misery. Be equally indifferent to both and abide in the faith of God. That will be so only when one's faith is strong that God looks after all of us.

Q. How shall I secure that firm faith?

M. Exactly. It is for such as these who want instructions. There are persons who seek freedom from misery. They are told that God guides all and so there need not be any concern about what happens. If they are of the best type they at once believe it and firmly abide by faith in God. But there are others who are not so easily convinced of the truth of the bare statement. They ask: "Who is God? What is His nature? Where is He? How can He be realised?" and so on. In order to satisfy them intellectual discussion is found necessary. Statements are made, their pros and cons are argued, and the truth is thus made clear to the intellect. When the matter is understood intellectually the earnest seeker begins to apply it practically. He argues at every moment, "For whom are these thoughts? Who am I?" and so forth, until he is well established in the conviction that a Higher Power guides us. That is firmness of faith. Then all his doubts are cleared and he needs no further instructions.

Q. We also have faith in God.

M. If it had been firm no questions would have arisen. The person will remain perfectly happy in his Faith in the Omnipotent.

Q. Is the enquiry into the Self the same as the above mentioned faith?

M. The enquiry into the Self is inclusive of all, faith, devotion, jnana [knowledge], yoga and all.

Q. A man sometimes finds that the physical body does not permit steady meditation. Should he practice yoga for training the body for the purpose?

M. It is according to one's innate predispositions [samskaras]. One man will practice hatha yoga for curing his bodily ills; another man will trust to God to cure them; a third man will use his will-power for it and a fourth man may be totally indifferent to them. But all of them will persist in meditation. The quest for the Self is the essential factor and all the rest are mere accessories. A man may have mastered the Vedanta philosophy and yet remain unable to control his thoughts. He may have a latent predisposition [purva samskara] which takes him to practice hatha yoga. He will believe that the mind can be controlled only by yoga and so he will practice it.

Q. What is most suitable for gaining facilities for steady dhyana? [meditation]

M. It depends on one's samskara [latent tendencies]. One may find hatha yoga suitable and another man nama japa, and so on. The essential point is the atma-vichara - enquiry into the Self.

Q. Is it enough if I spend some time in the mornings and

some time in the evenings for this atma-vichara? Or should I do it always - say, even when I am writing or walking?

M. Now what is your real nature? Is it writing, walking, or being? The one unalterable reality is Being. Until you realise that state of pure being you should pursue the enquiry. If once you are established in it there will be no further worry.
No one will enquire into the source of thoughts unless thoughts arise. So long as you think "I am walking," "I am writing," enquire who does it. These actions will however go on when one is firmly established in the Self. Does a man always say, "I am a man, I am a man, I am a man," every moment of his life? He does not say so and yet all his actions are going on.

Q. Is an intellectual understanding of the Truth necessary?

M. Yes. Otherwise why does not the person realise God or the Self at once, i.e., as soon as he is told that God is all or the Self is all? That shows some wavering on his part. He must argue with himself and gradually convince himself of the Truth before his faith becomes firm. [2]

27.

The Eloquence of Silence

Instead of giving instructions about his teaching verbally, Ramana Maharshi passed on his teaching almost exclusively through silence. That is, his presence, which radiated a state of stillness was powerful enough to awaken a serene inner stillness in many of those present.

Ramana's silence may need some explanation. Strange though it may seem, silence is an important means of communication. It can even be used in the field of language teaching. In 1963 psychologist, educator and mathematician, Caleb Gattegno introduced the 'Silent Way', a method of teaching languages in which the teacher remains silent in order to enhance student awareness. He demonstrated that awareness is fundamental in education. [1]

Ramana Maharshi outlined the origin of the use of silence and argued that teaching in silence is better than teaching by speaking.

On 30th January 1935 he answered a question about solitude raised by the American anthropologist Evans-Wentz who wrote the preface to Yogananda's '*Autobiography of a Yogi*.' Ramana Maharshi described the nature of his silence.

> M.   . . . By silence, eloquence is meant. Oral lectures are not so eloquent as silence. Silence is unceasing eloquence. [2]

On 8th September 1936 He described silence further.

> M.   Silence is ever-speaking; it is a perennial flow of

language; it is interrupted by speaking. These words obstruct that mute language. There is electricity flowing in a wire. With resistance to its passage, it glows as a lamp or revolves as a fan. In the wire it remains as electric energy. Similarly also, silence is the eternal flow of language, obstructed by words. [3]

The written recorded dialogues over three years in the book, 'Talks with Sri Ramana Maharshi,' show that he spoke on only 220 out of 1095 days; roughly once every five days which by any standard is virtual silence. When he did speak, it was to pass his teaching on to those who did not understand his silent teaching, which he regarded as more direct. His silent teaching is still regarded as the best today.

Ramana's decision to teach in silence may be more comprehensible when we consider that what he was teaching was inner stillness, that is the peace of having no thoughts, having transcended thought. Is there any better way to teach not having thoughts than by not thinking, not speaking and just being an example of having transcended thought? His teaching is beyond thought because it is experience of Awareness. It is transcending thought.

Even in the presence of a person with a long list of questions, Ramana Maharshi chose to communicate as usual through silence. The influence of Ramana Maharshi's silence is described most clearly regarding a woman who seemed inconsolable after the death of her husband.

A woman from the north of India had been swimming with her husband in the sea in Madras when in front of her eyes he was taken by a shark. She couldn't cope with it. She went everywhere seeing wise men and holy men to ask, 'What did we do wrong? Who did we harm? We married each other. We behaved correctly. Why?' She had found that many people had talked to her, but when she went out, she couldn't remember what they had said. They had used long phrases about the soul and spirituality. She wanted an answer. She visited the Osborne family in the southern town of Tiruvannamalai, whilst going to see Ramana Maharshi.

Katya Osborne, who was a young girl at that time told me of her experience. She said that she couldn't bear sitting with the woman because she was tense and wound up. Katya was asked to take the woman to see Ramana Maharshi and she showed the woman into the Hall where Ramana Maharshi sat.

At the sound of the lunch time bell, Katya went to get her to take her back home. When she got back to the hall Katya saw the woman and still recounts:

'She was at peace and I couldn't believe it. I couldn't believe that this was the same women that I couldn't bear to be with a couple of hours ago. So I wanted to ask her what he had said because I thought to myself, whatever he had said to her . . . those words must be the most important words in the World, they changed this woman completely, what are they, what did he say? I thought my mother will ask her, then I will find out. So, we came home and my mother did ask her what he said and the woman answered.

"Nothing." She had her list of questions which she took out. When he looked at her he looked so compassionate, she suddenly thought, "It doesn't matter." She left the list of questions and came out of the hall.'

The silent look of compassion this woman received had such a profound effect on her, that its impact was not only seen and felt by Katya when she collected her, but was still present when she told me about this woman. The impact it had on Katya then continues to be felt today when she shares this story along with others on YouTube. [4]

Ramana Maharshi was frequently asked about stillness and consciousness and on 11th April 1937 he was asked:

Q. How is the mind to be stilled?

M. Looking at the mind with the mind, or fixing the mind in the Self, brings the mind under control of the Self.

Q. Is there any yoga, i.e., a process for it?

M. Vichara [Self-enquiry] alone will do. [5]

On 21st December 1938 a saying of Lau Tzu from '*Tao Te Ching*' was read out in the hall which Ramana Maharshi responded to and explained:

"By his non-action the sage governs all."

M. Non-action is unceasing activity. The sage is characterised by eternal and intense activity. His stillness is like the apparent stillness of a fast-rotating top [gyroscope]. Its very speed cannot be followed by the eye and so it appears to be still. Yet it is rotating. So is the apparent inaction of the sage.

This must be explained because the people generally mistake stillness to be inertness. It is not so. [6]

28.

Silently Still

As we have just seen, the written recorded dialogues over three years in the book, 'Talks with Sri Ramana Maharshi,' show that he spoke on only 220 out of 1095 days; roughly once every five days which by any standard is virtual silence. This is quite an extraordinary minimal amount of speech.

Most of the dialogues recorded of Ramana Maharshi were made in the 'Old Hall' and are contained in the book *Talks with Sri Ramana Maharshi*, which was written by Munagala Venkataramiah, during the period between May 15th 1935 and 1st April 1939. [1]

Twice in the past I have borrowed Munagala Venkataramiah's original ledger book from the Sri Ramanasramam Archive in which he made his recordings in fountain pen. Each time I went through all the handwritten pages over several days.

I was so surprised Ramana Maharshi spoke so little that I decided to compare these records with two other recordings at other times in the Old Hall.

The two other recorders were intermittently present in the Old Hall between 1945 and 1949 and both made notes of what Ramana Maharshi said on the days on which they were present. Suri Nagamma wrote letters to her brother about what happened in front of Ramana Maharshi from 21st November 1945 to 24th December 1949. These were published in a book, *Letters from Sri Ramanasramam*, [2]

Devaraja Mudaliar recorded what Ramana Maharshi said between 16th March 1945 and 4th January 1947 in a book titled *Day by Day with Bhagavan*, [3]

These two recorder's time in the 'Old Hall' overlapped for over one year and they concur. There were few discrepancies between their two independent records. Their records confirm the few words Ramana Maharshi spoke on the days that he did speak.

However, what was most remarkable was that Ramana Maharshi's answers to all the questions asked of him, were answered directly and simply without any hesitation. There was no editing of the words he spoke or any changes to any of the written records.

29.

Discernment

The aim in following the path of Ramana Maharshi is to experience the happiness of the stillness of Being. Ignorance consists of thinking one is a collection of thoughts that constitute the ego. There is nothing to be added. The process consists solely in the subtraction of ignorance. The path to follow is Self-enquiry.

The only task is removal of your ignorance. When this has been achieved, there is no 'I' to say "I have achieved this" because the ego has been destroyed.

However, this initial realisation is usually only a temporary glimpse and it is therefore necessary to continue along your path with as much effort and humility as before.

Ignoring this and failing to continue to make effort risks believing the goal has already been attained.

On 19th January 1936 Ramana Maharshi, in response to a question from Mr. Ellappa Chettiar, a Member of the Legislative Council, from Salem, indicated that at first realisation is not usually permanent.

Q. Can jnana [Knowledge] be lost after being once attained?

M. Jnana, once revealed, takes time to steady itself. The Self is certainly within the direct experience of everyone, but not as one imagines it to be. It is only as it is. This Experience is samadhi [blissful meditative awareness]. [1]

Some individuals who have had a temporary 'glimpse' think they have reached their goal and achieved realisation. They may feel spiritually superior and they may subsequently begin teaching. This is a pitfall that often crops up when ignorance remains.

These individuals are susceptible to the cravings of their ego for attention. This is the very opposite of what they advocate for others.

No teacher is needed to follow the path of Ramana Maharshi.

No Successors

Ramana Maharshi is not well known because there is no promotion or advertising of him. He made no attempt to court celebrity. His teaching was and still is through silence. There is no sound recording of his voice. He did not leave any heirs or indicate successors to teach his way. When asked if someone should teach their knowledge to others, he was abundantly clear.

On 22nd September 1936 Ramana Maharshi was asked about teaching.

Q. Is a man to engage in teaching his knowledge however imperfect?

M. If his prarabdha [that part of one's karma which is to be worked out in this life] be that way.

In the seventh chapter, [of the Bhagavad Gita] Arjuna asks if Karma is a method [sadhana] [of spiritual practice]. Krishna answers that it is so if done without the sense of doership.

So also are Karmas approved by scriptures which deny Karma. The Karma disapproved by them is that which is done with the sense of doership. Do not leave Karma. You cannot do so. Give up the sense of doership. Karma will go on automatically. Or Karma will drop away from you. If Karma be your lot according to prarabdha, it will surely be done whether you will it or not; if Karma be not your lot, it will not be done even if you intently engage in it. Janaka, Suka, etc., were also in work without ahankara, Karma may be done for fame, or may be done unselfishly and for the public good. Yet even then they want applause. So it is really selfish. [2]

Doership is understood as having the feeling we are the doer, when all actions are regarded as being directed by cosmic law. Being directed by cosmic law is similar to Einstein's belief in Determinism.

Ramana Maharshi indicated he did not want anyone replacing him to pass on his teaching when he died. He said that he would always be present even when the body had gone. He did not appoint any successor, and none exists. However, there are a few quiet, unassuming people who, without wanting any attention, approval or praise, pass on what they know by pointing to the original words of Ramana Maharshi.

There are no teachers of his work as no intermediary is needed. It is as if he has shown exactly where the path is and it is up to you to be on it.

Grace or a Charismatic personality

There has been a surge of people acting as gurus as if it were a profession. In wanting to enhance their image, they frequently tell their followers: 'You are already Self-realised. It's just that you are not aware of it.' The result is that their followers then start to behave as if they are already Self-realised, when they have not yet realised the Self. Fortunately, when they notice this their guru's influence over them usually fizzles out.

Ramana Maharshi stated clearly that it is usually only with great effort that someone has their ignorance permanently removed.

He is found by attraction, not by promotion, that is by chance coming across a photograph, a mention in a book or by word of mouth.

Being in the presence of a realised person with charisma is different from being in the presence of someone with the traits of a 'charismatic personality.' Authentic charisma means 'grace' or 'favour freely given.' It involves giving with no desire to be rewarded in any way.

But someone with charismatic personality traits has a very different intention. The traits of a charismatic personality are social skills which can be learnt. There are thousands of psychologists and trainers who run courses to teach these skills such as competence, warmth, active listening and non-verbal communication.

Clever manipulative marketing can also make certain people or social media sites seem attractive so that we are cunningly lured into their illusion. Most sales departments give this kind of training to their staff to increase sales. Many internet sites give similar impressions.

Individuals who seek applause usually want to feed and expand their ego rather than to extinguish it. They tend to be charismatic individuals seeking adulation

Charismatic personalities may be confident and charming but they usually transmit more about their personality than inner stillness and compassion, which they usually lack. Inner stillness and ambition are usually incompatible.

Charismatic people's teachings are usually promoted by advertising which is paid for by services such as training courses or membership fees. There is almost always a catch somewhere when payment of money is involved.

Recognising a charismatic personality can be difficult and requires discernment and good judgement. When seeking help, you are often at your most vulnerable and consequently you may be lacking in discernment. That is, you may not be able to discriminate between good and bad influences on you.

Most importantly, distinguishing between *'grace,'* that is *assistance freely given* and someone charging money or wanting a favour in exchange, can also be difficult.

When you escape from being duped by a charismatic personality, perseverance helps you to uncover your inner awareness to find your own way to stay on the true path, which is also the goal.

Resetting the default away from thinking with only fleeting glances of oneness to more consistent awareness of the true inner Self is essential.

On 10th June 1936 Ramana Maharshi spoke about God and Guru in relation to the Self, describing them as both inside and outside the individual and not different from him. At first this may seem counterintuitive. However given that we are subject to the laws of Nature, it does make sense.

M. *Isvaro gururatmeti* ... [God is the same as Guru and Self ...]. A person begins with dissatisfaction. Not content with the world he seeks satisfaction of desires by prayers to God; his mind is purified; he longs to know God more than to satisfy his carnal desires. Then God's Grace begins to manifest. God takes the form of a Guru and appears to the devotee; teaches him the Truth; purifies the mind by his teachings and contact;

the mind gains strength, is able to turn inward; with meditation it is purified yet further, and eventually remains still without the least ripple. That stillness is the Self. The Guru is both exterior and interior. From the exterior he gives a push to the mind to turn inward; from the interior he pulls the mind towards the Self and helps the mind to achieve quietness. That is Grace. Hence there is no difference between God, Guru and Self. [3]

30.

The Bliss of No Want

On 17th March 1939 Ramana Maharshi said that happiness was only to be found inside and that it was peace.

M. If a man thinks that his happiness is due to external causes and his possessions, it is reasonable to conclude that his happiness must increase with the increase of possessions and diminish in proportion to their diminution. Therefore, if he is devoid of possessions, his happiness should be nil. What is the real experience of man? Does it conform to this view? [1]

He also said that there is no Happiness to be found in any worldly things.

M. 'What is happiness? Happiness is the very nature of the Self; happiness and the Self are not different. There is no happiness in any object of the world. We imagine through our ignorance that we derive happiness from objects. When the mind goes out, it experiences misery. In truth, when its desires are fulfilled, it returns to its own place and enjoys the happiness that is the Self. [2]

He added that the greatest happiness is 'the bliss of no want.'

M: I had no cloth spread on the floor in earlier days. I used to sit on the floor and lie on the ground. That is freedom. The sofa is a bondage. It is a gaol for me. I am not allowed to sit where and how I please. Is it not bondage? One must be free to do as one pleases and should not be served by others.

'No want' is the greatest bliss. It can be realised only by experience. Even an emperor is no match for a man with no want. [3]

31.

The Wound's Gift

Although most of us instinctively try to avoid suffering, it is often the case that the very suffering we seek to avoid is that which opens up the way to greater awareness. In particular, we may become aware that our existence goes far beyond our bodies, thoughts and feelings. The pain and suffering of a difficult time can in fact trigger inner glimpses of something greater, glimpses of an 'awareness of oneness with everything'.

Rumi, the 13th-century Sufi poet, was one of the first to understand the importance of pain and suffering. The following poem is attributed to him:

"I said: what about my eyes?

He said: Keep them on the road.

I said: What about my passion?

He said: Keep it burning.

I said: What about my heart?

He said: Tell me what you hold inside it?

I said: Pain and sorrow.

He said: Stay with it. The wound is the place

Where the light enters you."

Or, as Leonard Cohen puts it more recently in his song *Anthem*:

Ring the bells that still can ring
Forget your perfect offering
There is a crack, a crack in everything
That's how the light gets in [1]

A similar but less common experience may come, not from suffering, but from perception of the wonder of nature or feeling the love of another person. This is called a 'peak experience' moment.

Peak experiences are much less common than the brief glimpses of 'awareness of oneness with everything' produced by pain and suffering, because pain and suffering are more frequent in life.

Whether a brief glimpse of 'awareness of oneness with everything' is experienced through pain and suffering or through a peak experience, it can, of course, be ignored and allowed to fade away. Alternatively, having seen it fleetingly just once, there may be a desire for more of it, leading to the realisation that the sense of separateness is a barrier to natural happiness. Once exposed, this sense of not living fully can no longer be ignored, sparking a decision to continue searching for inner happiness. The delusion of separateness is seen through, paving the way for moving away from it in search of oneness.

In the past many more people than today used to turn to religion for inner happiness. Traditional religions were inspired by their founders' state of awareness. Religions originally showed how to experience this state. But they gradually ceased to do this and thus outlived their original purpose. Although a mystical element persists in many organized religions, it is generally to be found on the fringes of these establishments

When organized religion fails to reveal a pathway to experience an 'awareness of oneness with everything', people look elsewhere.

Most people commonly perceive themselves as separate from Nature, the universe, and their fellow human beings. This sense of separation creates a barrier to inner awareness. The absence of 'oneness with everything' perpetuates what Ramana Maharshi refers to as the 'everyday misery of mundane life'. The awareness of ignorance can be used as a friend and guide to gently reveal the way back to an 'awareness of oneness with everything'.

In 1950 Einstein illustrated the importance of the need to overcome the delusion of separateness to a rabbi who had lost his son. The rabbi had written to Einstein for help because he was distraught at the death of his 11-year-old son from polio. In his reply to the letter from the rabbi, Einstein points out the delusion of separateness.

Dear Dr. Einstein,

[. . .] I write you all this because I have just read your volume The World as I See It. On page 5 of that book you stated: "Any individual who should survive his physical death is beyond my comprehension... such notions are for the fears or absurd egoism of feeble souls." And I inquire in a spirit of desperation, is there in your view no comfort, no consolation for what has happened? Am I to believe that my beautiful darling child... has been forever wedded into dust, that there was nothing within him which has defied the grave and transcended the power of death? Is there nothing to assuage the pain of an unquenchable longing, an intense craving, an unceasing love for my darling son?

May I have a word from you? I need help badly.

Sincerely yours,
Robert S. Marcus [2]

Although the rabbi was a complete stranger, a few days later Einstein replied with words offering a fresh perspective.

February 12, 1950

Dear Dr Marcus:

A human being is part of the whole, called by us "Universe," a part limited in time and space. He experiences himself, his thoughts and feelings as something separated from the rest — a kind of optical delusion of his consciousness. The striving to free oneself from this delusion is the one issue of true religion. Not to nourish the delusion but to try to overcome it is the way to reach the attainable measure of peace of mind.

With my best wishes, sincerely yours,

Albert Einstein [3]

We do not know to what extent the rabbi found comfort in Einstein's words of stark realism and intellectual honesty. The rabbi's grief may be seen as an example of a wound that potentially opens the way to the removal of ignorance.

32.

Loss of a Child

Einstein points out to Rabbi Marcus that our main problem is that because of the orientation of our thoughts we have a false sense of separateness. This is our 'delusion of separateness.'

Experiencing our true Self, is blocked by our thinking. We are walled off.

Overcoming our separateness from our natural Happiness, 'our oneness with everything,' is beyond the scope of psychology but not beyond the scope of our awareness.

This is because psychology is limited by thinking and language, whereas Awareness has no such limitation. Awareness of a superior intelligent force behind nature is not limited by thoughts and words. This Awareness is knowing with certainty.

Both Einstein and Ramana Maharshi were men of considerable compassion. They had a deep understanding of the false sense of separateness and the difficulties it entails for the bereaved. But they had completely different ways of communicating

Einstein explained himself to the rabbi by means of a letter whilst Ramana Maharshi communicated by Being Still.

However, the most important difference between Einstein and Ramana Maharshi is that whilst Einstein was aware of our separateness, Ramana Maharshi was able to show us the way to end our separateness and to do it without religion and sometimes even without words.

It is worth revisiting the earlier story about his silence in the story of the woman whose husband had been killed by a shark.

Ramana Maharshi was able to give reassurance to the aggrieved widow. Katya Osborne tells how Ramana Maharshi was able to comfort her without saying a word.

When he looked at her he looked so compassionate, she suddenly thought, "It doesn't matter." She left the list of questions and came out of the hall.'

Ramana Maharshi understood the difficulty visitors had with understanding the false sense of separateness. From 1935-1936, 14 years before Einstein's letter to Rabbi Marcus, Ramana Maharshi spoke with three parents whose young children had died. In each case, he went to considerable length to explain our false sense of separateness.

The three examples all illustrate the misperception we have of who we are.

On 3rd October 1935 a very devoted and simple disciple had lost his only son, a child of three years. The next day he arrived at the Ashram with his family. Ramana Maharshi spoke with reference to them:

M. "Training of mind helps one to bear sorrows and bereavements with courage. But the loss of one's offspring is said to be the worst of all griefs. Grief exists only so long as one considers oneself to be of a definite form. If the form is transcended one will know that the one Self is eternal. There is no death nor birth. That which is born is only the body. The body is the creation of the ego. But the ego is not ordinarily perceived without the body. It is always identified with the body. It is the thought which matters. Let the sensible man consider if he knew his body in deep sleep. Why does he feel it in the waking state? But, although the body was not felt in sleep, did not the Self exist then? How was he in deep sleep? How is he when awake? What is the difference? Ego rises up and that is waking.

Simultaneously thoughts arise. Let him find out to whom are the thoughts. Wherefrom do they arise? They must spring up from the conscious Self. Apprehending it even vaguely helps the extinction of the ego. Thereafter the realisation of the one Infinite Existence becomes possible. In that state there are no individuals other than the Eternal Existence. Hence there is no thought of death or wailing. "If a man considers he is born he cannot avoid the fear of death. Let him find out if he has been born or if the Self has any birth. He will discover that the Self always exists, that the body which is born resolves itself into thought and that the emergence of thought is the root of all mischief. Find wherefrom thoughts emerge. Then you will abide in the ever present inmost Self and be free from the idea of birth or the fear of death." [1]

On 29th September 1936 a pensive, intelligent, aristocratic lady said to Ramana Maharshi:

Q. I shall be more definite. Though a stranger, I am obliged to confess the cause of my anxiety. I am blessed with children. A boy - a good brahmachari [celibate] - passed away in February. I was grief-stricken. I was disgusted with this life. I want to devote myself to spiritual life. But my duties as a housewife do not permit me to lead a retired life. Hence my doubt.

M. Retirement means abidance in the Self. Nothing more. It is not leaving one set of surroundings and getting entangled in another set, nor even leaving the concrete world and becoming involved in a mental world. The birth of the son, his death, etc., are seen in the Self only. Recall the state of sleep. Were you aware of anything happening? If the son or the world be real, should they not be present with you in sleep? You cannot deny your existence in sleep. Nor can you deny you were happy then. You are the same person now speaking and raising doubts. You are not happy, according to you. But you were happy in sleep.

119

What has transpired in the meantime that happiness of sleep has broken down? It is the rise of ego. That is the new arrival in the jagrat (waking) state. There was no ego in sleep. The birth of the ego is called the birth of the person. There is no other kind of birth. Whatever is born is bound to die. Kill the ego: there is no fear of recurring death for what is once dead. The Self remains even after the death of the ego. That is Bliss - that is Immortality.

    Q. How is that to be done?

    M. See for whom these doubts exist. Who is the doubter? Who is the thinker? That is the ego. Hold it. The other thoughts will die away. The ego is left pure; see wherefrom the ego arises. That is pure consciousness. [2]

On 5th November 1936 Ramana Maharshi answered a woman's question about grief following the death of her son. Again he reminds us that we feel separate because of misidentifying our Self.

    Q. . . Is it possible to know the condition of an individual after his death?

    M. It is possible. But why try to know it? All facts are only as true as the seeker.

    Q. The birth of a person, his being and death are real to us.

    M. Because you have wrongly identified your own self with the body, you think of the other one in terms of the body. Neither you are nor the other is the body.

    Q. But from my own level of understanding I consider myself and my son to be real.

M. The birth of the 'I-thought' is one's own birth, its death is the person's death. After the 'I-thought' has arisen the wrong identity with the body arises. Thinking yourself the body, you give false values to others and identify them with bodies. Just as your body has been born, grows and will perish, so also you think the other was born, grew up and died. Did you think of your son before his birth? The thought came after his birth and persists even after his death. Inasmuch as you are thinking of him he is your son. Where has he gone? He has gone to the source from which he sprang. He is one with you. So long as you are, he is there too. If you cease to identify yourself with the body, but see the real Self, this confusion will vanish. You are eternal. The others also will similarly be found to be eternal. Until this truth is realised there will always be this grief due to false values arising from wrong knowledge and wrong identity.
[3]

This is remarkably similar to the advice Einstein gave to the rabbi. Peace of mind can be achieved by overcoming the delusion of separateness.

By changing our awareness we are able to overcome what previously seemed like an insurmountable problem. We see it as part of us.

As we have mentioned, our ability to change our awareness of who we think we are seems to be most easily accessible when we are suffering.

Suffering is somehow able to activate our awareness. Suffering can waken us to the realisation that we are more than just our thoughts and feelings.

The pain and suffering of a difficult time can give glimpses of an 'awareness of oneness with everything,' of something greater than us.

121

The Swiss psychologist Carl Jung in his Commentary on *The Secret of the Golden Flower*, says of our insurmountable problems:

". . . all the greatest and most important problems of life are fundamentally insoluble . . . they can never be solved, but only outgrown." [4]

33.

The 'Direct' Path

Ramana Maharshi maintained that a person could attain Self-realisation by the practice of Self-enquiry. The principle question to ask is: 'Who am I?' However, he also said that there was another route. Practising the path of 'devotion' led to the same state of realisation of the Self, but that Self-enquiry is preferable for those who are ripe for it as of the two routes it is the more direct.

He said that if we repeatedly ask the question, 'Who am I?' eventually the Self and Guru and God will be seen as one and the same. So, what does this mean? It means that when, after persistent effort, we are able to be still with no thoughts, we experience the 'awareness of oneness with everything' and we experience with absolute certainty our true Self. It is impossible to convey this experience fully using language because it involves an inner experience.

The true Self is uncovered and recognised by conscious intuition. It is verifiable only by personal experience and not by theory or logic. It is experiential knowledge. That is why it is difficult even to attempt to describe it in words. When Ramana Maharshi did speak, it was almost always to pass his teaching on to those who did not respond to his silent teaching. But he always considered silent teaching to be preferable as he regarded it as more direct.

In asking 'Who am I?' you awaken to the realisation that you are not merely a bundle of thoughts, skin and bones called the Ego. This realisation is what is meant by having your 'Ignorance removed.' You are awakened to the truth of your existence. This awakening may initially be only a fleeting glimpse

A vital stage on the path of Sri Ramana Maharshi is this unveiling and recognition of the true Self.

This is not something that is obtained. Nothing is added to you. It is a process of subtraction. It is done by removal of illusion and ignorance. It is unlearning who you think you are and then seeing what you actually are, the Self, awareness. It is giving up the sense of being an 'I', as doer and simply being.

Ramana Maharshi's fundamental teaching is centered around asking, 'Who am I?' And just being.

34.

Who am I? Questions

Before going into greater detail about Ramana Maharshi's 'method' and teaching, a brief outline will be given of initial results commonly experienced by those who choose to follow the path of Self-enquiry.

When the question, 'Who am I?' is asked and answered the initial consideration generally focuses on the body and physical features and characteristics. These elements are usually considered first because the body is what people mostly identify with. Gradually, the body, the senses, and the brain can be excluded when it is realised that these things are not part of the true Self.

Next, it can be asked, 'WHO is asking this?' It might be noticed that the questioner is not the same as the ego, which is now perceived as a mere idea of body and thoughts. Thus, it is not the individual who is thinking but something greater, a higher level of Consciousness.

Then it can be asked, 'WHO or WHAT is this higher level of Consciousness?' It might become apparent that the entity is the Witness who has always been present, whether asleep or awake. Following this, the question 'WHO is this Witness?' might lead to the realization that it is Awareness.

By asking, 'WHO is the Awareness?' only Awareness remains. At some point, if the question is 'WHO is this Awareness?' then, 'Where does this Awareness, this I, come from?' there is no explanation for this higher Awareness. It is not the ego, an illusory collection of thoughts, thus it can only originate from a source previously unknown. This might lead to the realization that Awareness comes from Nature.

The question, 'Who am I?' can be asked again, but this time without the I, resulting in the realisation of 'Amness', unfathomable Being.

It may be perceived that this Amness originates from 'where everything comes from in Nature.' At any of these points, a glimpse of the non-existence of the I and the oneness with everything might be perceived. The lack of a name, form, or image does not matter.

By staying with Awareness and continually pushing thoughts away, the experience of oneness with everything might recur. This may occur soon after the initial glimpse or after a period of days, weeks, months, or years. How then can this state of oneness be retrieved and made more permanent?

35.

Awareness of Oneness of the Eternal 'I-I'

'I-I' is the name for the Self

On 21st October 1936 Ramana Maharshi went into great depth about the personal 'I' and the unity of 'I-I'.

He described how to transcend the personal 'I' to be aware of the oneness of the infinite eternal 'I-I'.

Q. How to attain the Self?

M. Self is not to be attained because you are the Self.

Q. Yes. There is an unchanging Self and a changing one in me. There are two selves.

M. The changefulness is mere thought. All thoughts arise after the arising of the 'I-thought'. See to whom the thoughts arise. Then you transcend them and they subside. This is to say, tracing the source of the 'I-thought', you realise the perfect 'I-I'. 'I' is the name of the Self . . .

M. After the rise of the 'I-thought' there is the false identification of the 'I' with the body, the senses, the mind, etc. 'I' is wrongly associated with them and the true 'I' is lost sight of. In order to shift the pure 'I' from the contaminated 'I' this discarding is mentioned. But it does not mean exactly discarding of the non-self, but it means the finding of the real Self. The real Self is the Infinite 'I-I', i.e., 'I' is perfection. It is eternal. It has no origin and no end. The other 'I' is born and also dies. It is impermanent. See to whom are the changing thoughts. They will be found to arise after the 'I-thought'. Hold the 'I-thought'. They subside. Trace back the source of the 'I-thought'. The Self alone will remain.

Q. It is difficult to follow. I understand the theory. But what is the practice?

M. The other methods are meant for those who cannot take to the investigation of the Self. Even to repeat Aham Brahmasmi [I am the ultimate reality or I am Brahman] or think of it, a doer is necessary. Who is it? It is 'I'. Be that 'I'. It is the direct method. The other methods also will ultimately lead everyone to this method of the investigation of the Self.

Q. I am aware of the 'I'. Yet my troubles are not ended.

M. This 'I-thought' is not pure. It is contaminated with the association of the body and senses. See to whom the trouble is. It is to the 'I-thought'. Hold it. Then the other thoughts vanish.

Q. Yes. How to do it? That is the whole trouble.

M. Think 'I' 'I' 'I' and hold to that one thought to the exclusion of all others. [1]

36.

Method and Truth

To understand the approach which Ramana Maharshi described as the 'direct path' and to understand what he said was 'truth,' it is best to look at them as he described them on several occasions.

Both 'truth' and 'method' are intertwined but for the purpose of understanding, we will examine them as separate entities.

On 20th February 1937 Ramana Maharshi gave insights into them both in answer to a single question.

Q. How is one to know the Self?

M. "Knowing the Self" means "Being the Self". . . 'Your duty is to be: and not to be this or that. "I AM that I AM" sums up the whole truth. The method is summed up in "BE STILL". What does "stillness" mean? It means "destroy yourself." Because any form or shape is the cause of trouble. Give up the notion that "I am so and so." [1]

Let us look first at what he means by the truth, summed up in a short sentence from the Old Testament. 'I AM that I AM.'

Truth

Ramana Maharshi was brought up as a Hindu but was educated in a Christian school, so it is not surprising that in helping us to answer the question, 'Who am I?' he quotes the Book of Exodus in the Old Testament [Exodus 3.14] When Moses asks the Burning Bush to tell the Israelites what the name of God is, the voice of God from the Burning bush replies, "I AM That I AM."

In using this quote 'I AM That I AM.' Ramana Maharshi means you must remove your false sense of who you are i.e. the bundle of thoughts comprising the ego and recognise your true Self, Awareness, 'That which is everything' . . . Brahman, the ultimate reality.

Ramana Maharshi did not believe in a personal God but in a God which is more in keeping with Brahman, the concept of God in the Vedanta Hindu philosophy. Brahman is the ultimate universal reality, the cause of everything that exists uniting everything, including Consciousness as a single binding unity.

He believed that Self, God and Guru are one and the same, beyond intellectual understanding and knowable only by direct experience. The block in perceiving this oneness is caused by the activity of the ego.

On 13th March 1936 he said:

M. The essence of mind is only awareness or consciousness. When the ego, however, dominates it, it functions as the reasoning, thinking or sensing faculty. The cosmic mind not being limited by the ego, has nothing separate from itself and is therefore only aware. This is what the Bible means by "I am that I AM".

The ego-ridden mind has its strength sapped and is too weak to resist the torturing thoughts. The egoless mind is happy in deep, dreamless sleep. Clearly therefore Bliss and misery are only modes of mind; but the weak mode is not easily interchangeable with the strong mode. Activity is weakness and consequently miserable; passivity is strength and therefore blissful. The dormant strength is not apparent and therefore not availed of.
The cosmic mind, manifesting in some rare being, is able to effect the linkage in others of the individual (weak) mind with

the universal (strong) mind of the inner recess. Such a rare being is called the GURU or God in manifestation. [2]

Method

Ramana Maharshi stated, "The method is summed up in "BE STILL" By being still Ramana Maharshi means having a mind that is still, with enhanced Awareness, as a result of having no thoughts.

Keeping thoughts away is achieved with perseverance. The mind accepts there is a higher state than that of having thoughts, which is being in a state of Awareness. This is uncovered by asking 'Who am I?'

On 23rd January 1937 Ramana Maharshi again explained both stillness and the answer to Who am I? together as they are both so intertwined.

M. The Bible says, "Be still and know that I am God". Stillness is the sole requisite for the realisation of the Self as God.

Q. Will the West ever understand this teaching?

M. There is no question of time and space. Understanding depends on ripeness of mind. What does it matter if one lives in the East or in the West? . . . Later Sri Bhagavan said the whole Vedanta is contained in two Biblical statements:

"I am that I AM" and "Be still and know that I am God." [3]

On 8th February 1937 he dismissed the delusory way in which we perceive ourselves as the doer.

M. Surrender once for all and be done with the desire. So long as the sense of doership is retained there is the desire; that is also personality. If this goes the Self is found to shine forth pure. The sense of doership is the bondage and not the actions themselves. "Be still and know that I am God." Here stillness is total surrender without a vestige of individuality. Stillness will prevail and there will be no agitation of mind. Agitation of mind is the cause of desire, the sense of doership and personality. If that is stopped there is quiet. There 'Knowing' means 'Being'. It is not the relative knowledge involving the triads, knowledge, subject and object.

Q. Is the thought "I am God" or "I am the Supreme Being" helpful?

M. "I am that I am." "I am" is God - not thinking, "I am God". Realise "I am" and do not think I am. "Know I am God" - it is said, and not "Think I am God."

Later Sri Bhagavan continued: It is said "I AM that I AM". That means a person must abide as the 'I'. He is always the 'I' alone. He is nothing else. Yet he asks, "Who am I?" A victim of illusion would ask "Who am I?" and not a man fully aware of himself. The wrong identity of the Self with the non-self makes you ask, "Who am I?"

Later still: There are different routes to Tiruvannamalai, but Tiruvannamalai is the same by whichever route it is gained. Similarly, the approach to the subject varies according to the personality. Yet the Self is the same. But still, being in Tiruvannamalai, if one asks for the route it is ridiculous. So also, being the Self, if one asks how to realise the Self it looks absurd. You are the Self. Remain as the Self. That is all. The questions arise because of the present wrong identification of the Self with the body. That is ignorance. This must go. On its removal the Self alone is. [4]

132

On 17th August 1938 he described reality as being the Self.

M. The only permanent thing is reality; and that is the Self. You say "I am", "I am going", "I am speaking", "I am working", etc. Hyphenate "I am" in all of them. Thus I - AM. That is the abiding and fundamental reality. This truth was taught by God to Moses: "I AM that I-AM". "Be still and know that I-AM God." so "I-AM" is God.

You know that you are. You cannot deny your existence at any moment of time. For you must be there in order to deny it. This [Pure Existence] is understood by stilling your mind. The mind is the outgoing faculty of the individual. If that is turned within, it becomes still in course of time and that "I-AM" alone prevails. "I-AM" is the whole Truth. [5]

On 1st February, 1939 Ramana Maharshi describes the limitation of the mind in being able to see its own source.

Q. When I go on analysing myself I go beyond the intellect, and then there is no happiness.

M. Intellect is only an instrument of the Self. It cannot help you to know what is beyond itself.

Q. I understand it. But there is no happiness beyond it.

M. The intellect is the instrument wherewith to know unknown things. But you are already known, being the Self which is itself knowledge; so you do not become the object of knowledge. The intellect makes you see things outside, and not that which is its own source.

Q. The question is repeated.

M . The intellect is useful thus far, it helps you to analyse

133

yourself, and no further. It must then be merged into the ego, and the source of the ego must be sought. If that be done the ego disappears. Remain as that source and then the ego does not arise. [6]

37.

The Alternative Method - The Path of Devotion

When Ramana Maharshi suggested the method of Self-enquiry he was careful to explain it was a subtraction. However, he also mentioned another path of subtraction to remove the ego.

Removal of ignorance, that is to say, of who you think you are, may be achieved when you realise that the ego is not you. Nothing is added to you when this takes place, because removing your ignorance is a subtraction. The result is 'being still.'

> M. The method is summed up in "BE STILL". What does "stillness" mean? It means "destroy yourself." Because any form or shape is the cause of trouble. Give up the notion that "I am so and so." [1]

Ramana Maharshi explained how to transcend the personal 'I' to be aware of the oneness of the infinite eternal 'I-I'. As we have seen, he said the ego mind could be destroyed by finding out who you are through Self-enquiry by asking 'Who am I?' This is seen as the path of 'knowledge' or the Direct Path.

Alternatively he said you could completely surrender by practicing the path of 'devotion.' He said it led to the same state of realisation of the Self. But he said that Self-enquiry, the path of knowledge was preferable for those who are ripe for it.

Whether you choose the path of knowledge or devotion, eventually they merge with each other and are seen as one and the same.

> M. There are only two ways to conquer destiny or be independent of it. One is to enquire for whom is this destiny and discover that only the ego is bound by destiny and not the

Self, and that the ego is non-existent. The other way is to kill the ego by completely surrendering to the Lord, by realising one's helplessness and saying all the time: 'Not I but Thou, oh Lord!', and giving up all sense of 'I' and 'mine' and leaving it to the Lord to do what he likes with you. Surrender can never be regarded as complete so long as the devotee wants this or that from the Lord. True surrender is love of God for the sake of love and nothing else, not even for the sake of salvation. In other words, complete effacement of the ego is necessary to conquer destiny, whether you achieve this effacement through jnana marga [path of self knowledge] or through bhakti-marga [path of devotion]. [2]

Surrender to Him and abide by His will whether he appears or vanishes; await His pleasure. If you ask Him to do as you please, it is not surrender but command to Him. You cannot have Him obey you and yet think that you have surrendered. He knows what is best and when and how to do it. Leave everything entirely to Him. His is the burden: you have no longer any cares. All your cares are His. Such is surrender. [3]

38.

No Teacher is Necessary

Ramana Maharshi specifies when a guru is necessary but also when a guru is not needed. He says the purpose of the guru is not to help us learn anything new but only to unlearn the orientations we have acquired. He is particularly clear that a guru does not have the power to liberate you.

On 16th November 1936 Ramana Maharshi spoke about the value of a teacher:

Q. Is there absolute necessity of a Guru for Self-Realisation?

M. So long as you seek Self-Realisation the Guru is necessary. Guru is the Self. Take Guru to be the Real Self and yourself as the individual self. The disappearance of this sense of duality is removal of ignorance. So long as duality persists in you the Guru is necessary. Because you identify yourself with the body you think the Guru, too, to be some body. You are not the body, nor is the Guru. You are the Self and so is the Guru. This knowledge is gained by what you call Self-Realisation. [1]

On 28th December 1937 a group of visitors asked the following questions.

Q. Is a teacher necessary for instructions?

M. Yes, if you want to learn anything new. But here you have to unlearn.

Q. Yet a teacher is necessary.

M. You have already got what you seek elsewhere. So no teacher is necessary.

Q. Is there any use of the man of realisation for the seeker?

M. Yes. He helps you to get rid of your delusion that you are not realised.

Q. So, tell me how.

M. The paths are meant only to de-hypnotise the individual. [2]

The Look of the Guru

Many people who follow the teachings of Ramana Maharshi say that they first became interested in him simply from seeing a photograph of him. Most commonly the photograph is the 1946 picture known as the *Welling Bust* which is at the front of this book between the picture of Einstein and page one.

Ramana Maharshi's look is not just one of friendly compassion or of love. In the eyes there is an extraordinary clarity. It is not just clarity of vision but clarity of an exceptionally rare kind.

When you look at his eyes, words are not necessary. You are drawn to his eyes because you are attracted to what he sees, which is an absence of separateness from everything, a oneness with everything. The photograph can be looked at like seeing the 'Self' in a mirror. In it we see what we are and we realise we too can remove our delusion of separateness. This is what draws us to Ramana Maharshi.

Seeing this look of 'oneness' when he was alive was no doubt the reason why many found it was unnecessary in his presence to

138

speak or ask him any questions.

Gajanan Govind Welling took the photograph in 1946. When he was about to take the photograph, Ramana Maharshi asked him if there was sufficient light. Welling answered. 'Bhagavan you are the light!'

In 1902 Ramana Maharshi was still in silence and only answered questions by writing down answers. This was the answer he gave to a question about God and Guru whilst he was living in Virupaksha Cave, one of several caves he lived in until 1922.

Q. Is it not possible for God and the Guru to effect the liberation of a soul?

M. God and the Guru will only show the way to liberation; they will not by themselves take the soul to the state of liberation. In truth, God and the Guru are not different. Just as the prey which has fallen into the jaws of a tiger has no escape, so those who have come within the ambit of the Guru's gracious look will be saved by the Guru and will not get lost; yet, each one should, by his own effort pursue the path shown by God or Guru and gain liberation. One can know oneself only with one's own eye of knowledge, and not with somebody else's. Does he who is Rama require the help of a mirror to know that he is Rama? [3]

39.

Effort and Perseverance

On 4th February 1935 Ramana Maharshi stressed the importance of applying effort and perseverance in order to give up the false 'I'.

A. . . . You give up this and that of 'my' possessions. If you give up 'I' and 'Mine' instead, all are given up at a stroke. The very seed of possession is lost. Thus the evil is nipped in the bud or crushed in the germ itself. Dispassion [vairagya] must be very strong to do this. Eagerness to do it must be equal to that of a man kept under water trying to rise up to the surface for his life.

Q. Cannot this trouble and difficulty be lessened with the aid of a Master or an Ishta Devata [God chosen for worship]? Cannot they give the power to see our Self as it is - to change us into themselves - to take us into Self-Realisation?

A. Ishta Devata and Guru are aids - very powerful aids on this path. But an aid to be effective requires your effort also. Your effort is a *sine qua non*. It is you who should see the sun. Can spectacles and the sun see for you? You yourself have to see your true nature. Not much aid is required for doing it! [1]

On 15th July 1935 Ramana Maharshi answered a problem posed in a letter. He pointed out that the problem was differentiating the false 'I' from the real 'I'. He said that effort was then needed to remove our ignorance.

M. One's efforts are directed only to remove one's ignorance. Afterwards they cease, and the real Self is found to be always there. No effort is needed to remain as the Self. [2]

On 23rd February 1937 Ramana Maharshi was answering some questions to a group of three people from Andhra Pradesh about meditation.

Q. How to meditate?

M. Concentrate on that one whom you like best. If a single thought prevails, all other thoughts are put off and finally eradicated. So long as diversity prevails there are bad thoughts. When the object of love prevails only good thoughts hold the field. Therefore hold on to one thought only. Dhyana is the chief practice.

Dhyana [meditation] means fight. As soon as you begin meditation other thoughts will crowd together, gather force and try to sink the single thought to which you try to hold. The good thought must gradually gain strength by repeated practice. After it has grown strong the other thoughts will be put to flight. This is the battle royal always taking place in meditation. One wants to rid oneself of misery. It requires peace of mind, which means absence of perturbation owing to all kinds of thoughts. Peace of mind is brought about by dhyana alone. [3]

On 14th April 1937 Ramana Maharshi said categorically that perseverance was needed to succeed.

Q. How can the rebellious mind be brought under control?

M. Either seek its source so that it may disappear or surrender that it may be struck down.

Q. But the mind slips away from our control.

M. Be it so. Do not think of it. When you recollect yourself bring it back and turn it inward. That is enough. No one succeeds without effort. Mind control is not one's birthright.

The successful few owe their success to their perseverance. A passenger in a train keeps his load on the head by his own folly. Let him put it down: he will find the load reaches the destination all the same. Similarly, let us not pose as the doers, but resign ourselves to the guiding Power. [4]

Although Ramana Maharshi supported and encouraged various methods to aid concentration in order to 'be still,' such as using a mantra or breathing methods, he stated clearly that they were aids and not essential, adding that he never used either.

On October 4th 1946 he was asked by Prof D. S. Sarma if he had a period of Sadhana [daily spiritual practice] in his life.

M.   I know of no such period. I never performed any Pranayama [method of breathing] or Japa [mantra]. I know no mantras. I had no rules of meditation or contemplation. Even when I came to hear of such things later, I was never attracted by them. Even now my mind refuses to pay any attention to them. Sadhana implies an object to be gained and the means of gaining it. What is there to be gained which we do not already possess? In meditation, concentration and contemplation, what we have to do is only, not to think of anything but to be still. Then we shall be in our natural state. This natural state is given many names — Moksha, [liberation] Jnana, [Self Knowledge] Atma, [the Self] etc. — and these give rise to many controversies. There was a time when I used to remain with my eyes closed. That does not mean that I was practising any Sadhana then. Even now I sometimes remain with my eyes closed. If people choose to say that I am doing some Sadhana at the moment, let them say so. It makes no difference to me. People seem to think that by practising some elaborate Sadhana the Self would one day descend upon them as something very big and with tremendous glory and they would then have what is called Sakshatkaram [direct perception of the Self]. The Self is Sakshat [direct] all right, but there is no karam or kirtam [doing or describing] about it. The word karam implies one's doing something. [5]

40.

Reality and the Removal of the Unreal

On 4th February 1935 Ramana Maharshi was asked about reality.

Q. What is the nature of the Reality?

M. Existence without beginning or end - eternal. Existence everywhere, endless, infinite. Existence underlying all forms, all changes, all forces, all matter and all spirit. The many change and pass away [phenomena], whereas the One always endures [noumenon].

The one displacing the triads, i.e., the knower, the knowledge and the known. The triads are only appearances in time and space, whereas the Reality lies beyond and behind them. They are like a mirage over the Reality. They are the result of delusion. [1]

On 24th January, 1938 Ramana Maharshi was asked about illusion.

Q. Are there degrees of illusion?

M. Illusion is itself illusory. Illusion must be seen by one beyond it. Can such a seer be subject to illusion? Can he then speak of degrees of illusion? There are scenes floating on the screen in a cinema show. Fire appears to burn buildings to ashes. Water seems to wreck vessels. But the screen on which the pictures are projected remains unscorched and dry. Why? Because the pictures are unreal and the screen is real. Again reflections pass through a mirror; but the mirror is not in any way affected by the quality or quantity of the reflections on it. So the world is a phenomenon on the single Reality, which is not affected in any manner. Reality is only one. The discussion about illusion is due to the difference in the angle of vision. Change your angle of vision to one of jnana and then find the universe to be only Brahman. Being now in the world, you see the world as such. Get beyond it and this will disappear: the Reality alone will shine. [2]

In February 1935 Ramana Maharshi was asked about reality and if the World is real or unreal?

Q. "The Supreme Spirit [Brahman] is Real. The world is illusion," is the stock phrase of Sri Sankaracharya. Yet others say, "The world is reality". Which is true?

M. Both statements are true. They refer to different stages of development and are spoken from different points of view. The abhyasi [aspirant] starts with the definition, that which is real exists always; then he eliminates the world as unreal because it is changing. It cannot be real; 'not this, not this!' The seeker ultimately reaches the Self and there finds unity as the prevailing note. Then, that which was originally rejected as being unreal is found to be a part of the unity. Being absorbed in the Reality, the world also is Real. [3]

During 1935 Ramanananda Swarnagiri wrote down some of the conversations he and some of his friends had with Ramana Maharshi.

Q. It is stated that the existence of the world is false, an illusion, Maya, but we see the world day after day. How can it be false?

M. By false it is meant that the conception of the world is a superimposition on reality, as the idea of a snake is superimposed on the reality of a rope, in darkness [in ignorance]. That is Maya, illusion.

144

Q. What is Maya? Illusion?

M. Seeing ice without seeing that it is water is illusion, Maya. Therefore saying things like killing the mind or anything like that also has no meaning, for after all mind also is part and parcel of the Self. Resting in the Self or inhering in the Self is mukti, [liberation] getting rid of Maya. Maya is not a separate entity. Absence of light is called darkness, so also absence of Knowledge, Illumination etc., is called ignorance, illusion or Maya. [4]

Major Chadwick recorded a conversation Ramana Maharshi had with him about doing things and being 'the doer.'

M. Why do you think that you are the doer? There lies all the trouble. It is quite absurd, as it is obvious to all that 'I' does nothing. It is only the body that acts, 'I' is always the witness. We so associate ourselves with our thoughts and actions that we continually say, 'I did this or that,' when we did nothing at all. Concentrate on being the witness and let things take their course, they will go on anyhow, you cannot prevent them. [5]

On 2nd May 1938 Ramana Maharshi again used the analogy of a cinema screen to show how the Self is Unaffected by Other States.

M. . . . Who is this 'I'? It cannot be the body nor the mind as we have seen before. This 'I' is the one who experiences the waking, dream and sleep states. The three states are changes which do not affect the individual. The experiences are like pictures passing on a screen in the cinema. The appearance and disappearance of the pictures do not affect the screen. So also, the three states alternate with one another leaving the Self unaffected. The waking and the dream states are creations of the mind. So the Self covers all. To know that the Self remains happy in its perfection is Self-Realisation. Its use lies in the realisation of Perfection and thus of Happiness. [6]

On 2nd May 1938 Ramana Maharshi talked about the immortal Self.

M. . . . The fear of death is of the body. It is not true of the Self. Such fear is due to ignorance. Realisation means True Knowledge of the Perfection and Immortality of the Self. Mortality is only an idea and cause of misery. You get rid of it by realising the Immortal nature of the Self. [7]

Universal Consciousness

A group of visitors was asking about the method of Realisation. On 4th May 1938, in the course of a reply, Sri Bhagavan spoke about Universal Consciousness:

M. Holding the mind and investigating it is advised for a beginner. But what is mind after all? It is a projection of the Self. See for whom it appears and from where it rises. The 'I-thought' will be found to be the root-cause. Go deeper; the 'I-thought' disappears and there is an infinitely expanded 'I-consciousness'. That is otherwise called Hiranyagarbha [Universal consciousness]. When it puts on limitations it appears as individuals. [8]

On 1st February 1939 Ramana Maharshi said that the absence of thoughts is progress towards realisation

M. The degree of the absence of thoughts is the measure of your progress towards Self-Realisation. But Self-Realisation itself does not admit of progress; it is ever the same. The Self remains always in realisation. The obstacles are thoughts. Progress is measured by the degree of removal of the obstacles

146

to understanding that the Self is always realised. So thoughts must be checked by seeking to whom they arise. So you go to their Source, where they do not arise. [9]

On 19th July 1946 Ramana Maharshi said that the means have to be of the nature of the Self. [the path is also the goal]

M. What is gayatri? [a mantra] It really means: "Let me concentrate on that which illumines all." Dhyana [concentration] really means only concentrating or fixing the mind on the object of dhyana. But meditation is our real nature. If we give up other thoughts what remains is 'I' and its nature is dhyana or meditation or jnana, whichever we choose to call it. What is at one time the means later becomes the end; unless meditation or dhyana were the nature of the Self it could not take you to the Self. If the means were not of the nature of the goal, it could not bring you to the goal. [10]

41.

Does Knowledge of Scriptures help?

As we saw in Einstein's letter to Dr Marcus the essential function of religion should be to help us remove our delusion of separateness and to show us how to experience an awareness of 'oneness with everything.'

We used to look for inner happiness in a religion, because that was where we were told happiness could be found. Each traditional religion was inspired by one person's original transcendental state of experiencing a feeling of *'awareness of oneness with everything.'*

Religions originated to show how to experience this Awareness. But now, no longer teaching how to experience the Awareness for which they were created, religions have largely outlived their original purpose. If you knock on the door of religion and do not find what you expect from it, you look elsewhere.

In 1959 the British born writer Arthur Osborne wrote a book *'The Rhythm of History.'* It was unusual because it was about the historical rhythms of the different forms of 'spirituality' in civilisations from their beginnings. He looked back at the introduction of religions to civilisations in the east and the west and he also looked at their gradual decline. He concluded that they showed similar patterns. Soon after their origins, religions quickly reached their peak only to go into a long decline. At their inception most of them predicted a time in the future when mankind would face a great crisis. [1]

Visitors who came to see Ramana Maharshi professed a wide variety of religious beliefs. Some were still deeply religious whilst others had given up the religion they were born into. He was frequently asked about the study of the Scriptures.

On 3rd July 1936 a visitor asked Ramana Maharshi if the study of the sacred books will reveal the Truth.

M. That will not suffice.

Q. Why not?

M. Samadhi [blissful meditative awareness] alone can reveal it. Thoughts cast a veil over reality and so it cannot be clear in states other than Samadhi.

Q. Is there thought in Samadhi? Or is there not?

M. There will only be the feeling 'I am' and no other thoughts.

Q. Is not 'I am' a thought?

M. The egoless 'I am' is not thought. It is realisation. The meaning or significance of 'I' is God. The experience of 'I am' is to Be Still. [2]

A few days later on 20th July 1936 he was asked a similar question about the Scriptures and religious books.

Q. Can one realise the Truth by learning the scriptures and study of books?

M. No. So long as predispositions remain latent in the mind, realisation cannot be achieved. Scripture learning is itself a predisposition of the mind. Realisation is only in samadhi, [blissful meditative awareness] [3]

On 28th June 1946 a woman appealed to him in writing asking if knowledge of the Scriptures is necessary to know the Self.

Q. I am not learned in the Scriptures and I find the method of Self-enquiry too hard for me. I am woman with seven children and a lot of household cares, and it leaves me little time for meditation. I request Bhagavan to give me some simpler and easier method.

M. No learning or knowledge of scriptures is necessary to know the Self, as no man requires a mirror to see himself. All knowledge is required only to be given up eventually as not-Self. Nor is household work or cares with children necessarily an obstacle. If you can do nothing more, at least continue saying 'I, I' to yourself mentally all the time, as advised in Who am I?, whatever work you may be doing and whether you are sitting, standing or walking. 'I' is the name of God. It is the first and greatest of all mantras. Even OM is second to it. [4]

Limitations of the Intellect, Psychology and Analysis

In February 1935 Ramana Maharshi was asked if studying Psychology or Philosophy was helpful?

Q. Is the study of science, psychology, physiology, philosophy, etc. helpful for:

(1) this art of yoga-liberation.
(2) the intuitive grasp of the unity of the Real?

M. Very little. Some knowledge is needed for yoga and it may be found in books. But practical application is the thing needed, and personal example, personal touch and personal instructions are the most helpful aids. As for the other, a person may laboriously convince himself of the truth to be intuited, i.e., its function and nature, but the actual intuition is akin to feeling and requires practice and personal contact. Mere book learning is not of any great use. After realisation, all intellectual loads are useless burdens and are thrown overboard as jetsam. Jettisoning the ego is necessary and natural. [1]

On 7th January 1935 Ramana Maharshi said that intellectual understanding had to be transcended.

Q. Should I remain as if in sleep and be watchful at the same time?

M. Yes. Watchfulness is the waking state. Therefore, the state will not be one of sleep, but sleepless sleep. If you go the way of your thoughts, you will be carried away by them and you will find yourself in an endless maze.

Q. So, then, I must go back tracing the source of thoughts.

M. Quite so; in that way the thoughts will disappear and the Self alone will remain. In fact there is no inside or outside for the Self. They are also projections of the ego. The Self is pure and absolute.

Q. It is understood intellectually only. Is not intellect a help for realisation?

M. Yes, up to a certain stage. Even so, realise that the Self transcends the intellect — the latter must itself vanish to reach the Self. [2]

On 10th April 1937 Ramana Maharshi pointed out that philosophy created confusion where none exists.

Q. A highly learned visitor whose chief interest was man and his constitution, wanted Sri Bhagavan to explain from experience man's various bodies, his koshas [layers of being] and their functions, his atma [self or soul]-buddhi [intellect]-manas, [human processing mind] etc.

M. The intricate maze of philosophy of different schools claims to clarify matters and reveal the Truth, but in fact they create confusion where no confusion need exist. To understand anything there must needs be the understanding being. Why worry about his bodies, his ahankar, his buddhi, creation, God, Mahatmas [enlightened person], world – the not-Self – at all? Why not remain yourself and be in peace? Take Vedanta, for instance: it speaks of the fifteen pranas, [life force] the names and functions of which the student is asked to commit to memory. Will it not be sufficient if he is taught that only one prana does the whole work of maintaining life in the body?

Again, the antahkarana [total mind] is said to think, to desire, to will, to reason, etc. Why all these details? Has anyone seen the antahkarana, or all these pranas? Do they really exist? They are all conceptual divisions invented by teachers of philosophy by their excessive analysis. Where do all these concepts end? Why should confusion be created and then explained away? Fortunate is the man who does not lose himself in the labyrinths of philosophy but goes straight to the Source from which they all rise. [3]

On 14th August 1938 Ramana Maharshi said the purpose of the intellect is to realise its own dependence upon the Higher Power.

Q. How is the mind to be steadily kept right?

M. All living beings are aware of their surroundings and therefore intellect must be surmised in all of them. At the same time, there is a difference between the intellect of man and that of other animals, because man not only sees the world as it is and acts accordingly, but also seeks fulfilment of desires and is not satisfied with the existing state of affairs. In his attempt to fulfil his desires he extends his vision far and wide and yet he turns away dissatisfied. He now begins to think and reason. The desire for permanency of happiness and of peace bespeaks such permanency in his own nature. Therefore, he seeks to find and regain his own nature, i.e., his Self. That found, all is found. Such inward seeking is the path to be gained by man's intellect. The intellect itself realises after continuous practice that it is enabled by some Higher Power to function. It cannot itself reach that Power. So it ceases to function after a certain stage. When it thus ceases to function the Supreme Power is still left there all alone. That is Realisation; that is the finality; that is the goal.

It is thus plain that the purpose of the intellect is to realise its own dependence upon the Higher Power and its inability to reach the same. So it must annihilate itself before the goal is gained. [4]

On 16th December 1938 Ramana Maharshi said that we need convincing of the Truth.

Q. Is an intellectual understanding of the Truth necessary?

M. Yes. Otherwise, why does not the person realise God or the Self at once, i.e., as soon as he is told that God is all or the Self is all? That shows some wavering on his part. He must argue with himself and gradually convince himself of the Truth before his faith becomes firm. [5]

On 3rd March 1939 Ramana Maharshi said that the purpose of the intellect is to show the way to the Self.

M. All knowledge is meant only to lead the person to the realisation of the Self. The scriptures or religions are well-known to be for that purpose. What do they all mean? Leave alone what they say of the past or of the future; for it is only speculative. But the present existence is within the experience of all. Realise the pure Being. There is an end to all discourses and disputes. But the intellect of man does not easily take to this course. It is only rarely that a man becomes introverted. The intellect delights in investigating the past and the future but does not look to the present.

Q. Because it must lose itself if it sank within in search of the Self. But the other investigation gives it not only a lease of life but also food for growth.

M. Yes. Quite so. Why is intellect developed? It has a purpose. The purpose is that it should show the way to realise the Self. It must be put to that use. [6]

On 1st February 1939 Ramana Maharshi emphasised remaining at that which is the source of the intellect.

Q. When I go on analysing myself I go beyond the intellect, and then there is no happiness.

M. Intellect is only an instrument of the Self. It cannot help you to know what is beyond itself.

Q. I understand it. But there is no happiness beyond it.

M. The intellect is the instrument wherewith to know unknown things. But you are already known, being the Self which is itself knowledge; so you do not become the object of knowledge. The intellect makes you see things outside, and not that which is its own source.

Q. [The question is repeated.]

M. The intellect is useful thus far, it helps you to analyse yourself, and no further. It must then be merged into the ego, and the source of the ego must be sought. If that be done the ego disappears. Remain as that source and then the ego does not arise. [7]

On 8th November 1945 Ramana Maharshi said the mind has to turn inwards to seek its own source.

Q. Is asking the mind to turn inward and seek its source not also employing the mind?

M. Of course we are employing the mind. It is well known and admitted that only with the help of the mind the mind has to be killed. But instead of setting about saying there is a mind, and I want to kill it, you begin to seek the source of the mind, and you find the mind does not exist at all. The mind, turned outwards, results in thoughts and objects. Turned inwards, it becomes itself the Self. [8]

43.

Self-enquiry or Meditation?

On 6th April 1937 Ramana Maharshi said 'Vichara [enquiry] is the process and also the goal. 'I AM' is the goal and the final reality.' Essentially he is saying that the path itself is also the goal. In other words, being on the path is the goal.

Q. When I read Sri Bhagavan's works I find that investigation is said to be the one method for Realisation.

M. Yes, that is vichara [enquiry].

Q. How is that to be done?

M. The questioner must admit the existence of his Self. "I AM" is the Realisation. To pursue the clue till Realisation is vichara. Vichara and Realisation are the same.

Q. It is elusive. What shall I meditate upon?

M. Meditation requires an object to meditate upon, whereas there is only the subject without the object in vichara. Meditation differs from vichara in this way.

Q. Is not dhyana [meditation] one of the efficient processes for Realisation?

M. Dhyana is concentration on an object. It fulfils the purpose of keeping away diverse thoughts and fixing the mind on a single thought, which must also disappear before Realisation. But Realisation is nothing new to be acquired. It is already there, but obstructed by a screen of thoughts. All our attempts are directed for lifting this screen and then Realisation is revealed. If a true seeker is advised to meditate, many may go away satisfied with the advice. But someone among them may turn round and ask, "Who am I to meditate on an object?" Such a one must be told to find the Self. That is the finality. That is Vichara.

Q. Will vichara alone do in the absence of meditation?

A. Vichara is the process and the goal also. 'I AM' is the goal and the final reality. To hold to it with effort is vichara. When spontaneous and natural it is Realisation. [1]

44.

Einstein's Genius as understood by Ramana Maharshi

Disbelief in Free Will

On 5th April 1937 Ramana Maharshi was asked about Einstein.

M. "There is nothing new under the sun." What we call inventions or discoveries are merely rediscoveries by competent men with strong samskara [latent tendencies] in the directions under consideration.

Q. Is it so with Newton, Einstein, etc.?

M. Yes. Certainly. But the samskaras, however strong, will not manifest unless in a calm and still mind. It is within the experience of everyone that his attempts to rake up his memory fail, whereas something flashes in the mind when he is calm and quiet. Mental quiet is necessary even for remembrance of forgotten things. The so-called genius is one who worked hard in his past births and acquired knowledge and kept it in store as samskaras. He now concentrates his mind until it merges in the subject. In that stillness the submerged ideas flash out. That requires favourable conditions also. [1]

3rd January 1936 Ramana Maharshi said that not identifying with the body frees us from the consequences of what the body does.

Q. "If there is a certain work destined to be done by each and we shall eventually do it however much we do not wish to do it or refuse to do it, is there any free will?"

M. "It is true that the work meant to be done by us will

be done by us. But it is open to us to be free from the joys or pains, pleasant or unpleasant consequences of the work, by not identifying ourselves with the body or that which does the work. If you realise your true nature and know that it is not you that does any work, you will be unaffected by the consequences of whatever work the body may be engaged in according to destiny or past karma or divine plan, however you may call it. You are always free and there is no limitation of that freedom."
[2]

On 3rd June 1936 Ramana Maharshi said that Jnana [wisdom] transcends free will and destiny.

M. Free-will and destiny are ever-existent. Destiny is the result of past action; it concerns the body. Let the body act as may suit it. Why are you concerned with it? Why do you pay attention to it? Free-will and Destiny last as long as the body lasts. But wisdom [jnana] transcends both. The Self is beyond knowledge and ignorance. Should anything happen, it happens as the result of one's past actions, of divine will and of other factors. [3]

On 19th June, 1936 Mr. B. C. Das, the physics lecturer, asked about free-will and destiny.

M. Whose will is it? 'It is mine', you may say. You are beyond will and fate. Abide as that and you transcend them both. That is the meaning of conquering destiny by will. Fate can be conquered. Fate is the result of past actions. By association with the wise the bad tendencies are conquered. One's experiences are then viewed to their proper perspective. I exist now. I am the enjoyer. I enjoy fruits of action. I was in the past and shall be in the future. Who is this 'I'? Finding this 'I' to be pure Consciousness beyond action and enjoyment, freedom and happiness are gained. There is then no effort, for the Self is perfect and there remains nothing more to gain. So long as there is individuality, one is the enjoyer and doer. But if it is lost, the divine Will prevails and guides the course of events. The individual is perceptible to others who cannot perceive divine force. Restrictions and discipline are for other individuals and not for the liberated. Free-will is implied in the scriptural injunctions to be good. It implies overcoming fate. It is done by wisdom. The fire of wisdom consumes all actions. Wisdom is acquired by association with the wise, or rather, its mental atmosphere. [4]

On 12th June 1937 Ramana Maharshi repeated that not identifying with the body frees us from consequences of what the body does.

Q. Has man any Free-Will or is everything in his life predestined and preordained?

M. Free-Will holds the field in association with individuality. As long as individuality lasts so long there is Free-Will. All the sastras [scriptures] are based on this fact and they advise directing the Free-Will in the right channel. Find out to whom Free-Will or Destiny matters. Abide in it. Then these two are transcended. That is the only purpose of discussing these questions. To whom do these questions arise? Find out and be at peace.

Q. Are intellect and emotion, like the physical body, growths which come with the birth of man; and do they dissolve or survive after death?

M. Before considering what happens after death, just consider what happens in your sleep. Sleep is only the interval between two waking states. Do they survive that interval?

Q. Yes, they do.

M. The same holds good for death also. They represent body consciousness and nothing more. If you are the body they always hold on to you. If you are not the body they do not affect you. The one who was in sleep is now in waking state just speaking. You were not the body in sleep. Are you the body now? Find it out. Then the whole problem is solved.

Similarly, that which is born must die. Whose is the birth? Were you born? If you say you were, of whose birth are you speaking? It is the body which was born and it is that which will die. How do birth and death affect the eternal Self? Think and say to whom the questions arise. Then you will know. [5]

On 28th June 1946 Ramana Maharshi said to conquer destiny you must either enquire to whom it is for or surrender by saying all the time: 'Not I Lord but Thou'.

Q. Is there destiny? And if what is destined to happen will happen is there any use in prayer or effort or should we just remain idle?

M. There are only two ways to conquer destiny or be independent of it. One is to enquire for whom is this destiny and discover that only the ego is bound by destiny and not the Self, and that the ego is non-existent. The other way is to kill the ego by completely surrendering to the Lord, by realizing one's helplessness and saying all the time: 'Not I but Thou, oh Lord!', and giving up all sense of 'I' and 'mine' and leaving it to the Lord to do what he likes with you. Surrender can never be regarded as complete so long as the devotee wants this or that from the Lord. True surrender is love of God for the sake of love and nothing else, not even for the sake of salvation. In other words, complete effacement of the ego is necessary to conquer destiny, whether you achieve this effacement through Self-enquiry or through bhakti-marga [path of devotion]. [6]

Ramana Maharshi and Einstein showed a remarkable disregard for the danger of death as demonstrated in their actions. Their behaviour was in keeping with their belief in predetermination.

Einstein demonstrated this on two occasions we have already seen.

The first was his hobby of sailing which was one of his greatest pleasures, second only to playing the violin. Einstein's behaved with a complete disregard for the threat of death. Although he was a non-swimmer, Einstein always refused to carry lifejackets on his sailing-boat.

The second was Einstein's apparent lack of concern about well published death threats. On January 30th 1933, Hitler became Chancellor of Germany. A few weeks later in March 1933, Einstein who was on a lecture tour of the United States, criticised Hitler's repressive government.

On March 28th 1933 Einstein moved to Belgium where he handed in his German passport at the German Consulate in Brussels and immediately renounced his German citizenship. Subsequently, Einstein's scientific works were publicly burned in Berlin and he was accused of spreading Communist propaganda. One German publication published a photograph of Einstein with the caption 'not yet hanged.' Einstein seemed unconcerned about the danger. This prompted his wife Elsa Einstein to insist they leave Belgium. After a great deal of persuasion from Elsa they left Belgium and arrived in Britain in early September 1933.

Ramana Maharshi also had a similar disregard for the threat of danger and death. This account was given by a retired lawyer, B.V. Narasimha Swami.

At 11.30 pm on June 26th 1924, thieves broke into the Ashram and smashed the glass panes of a window. They then mercilessly beat Ramana Maharshi who sat calmly. They also beat his attendants. He said, 'Let them play their role; we shall stick to ours. Let them do what they like. It is for us to bear and forebear. Let us not interfere with them.' eventually the thieves left. [7]

162

45.

Morality

On 4th May 1937 a book was read in which the question arose of whether the world was created for happiness or misery. All eyes turned to Sri Bhagavan for the answer.

M. Creation is neither good nor bad; it is as it is. It is the human mind which puts all sorts of constructions on it, as it sees things from its own angle and as it suits its own interests. A woman is just a woman, but one mind calls her "mother," another "sister," and still another "aunt" and so on. Men love women, hate snakes, and are indifferent to the grass and stones by the roadside. These connections are the causes of all the misery in the world. Creation is like a peepul tree: birds come to eat its fruit, or take shelter under its branches, men cool themselves in its shade, but some may hang themselves on it. Yet the tree continues to lead its quiet life, unconcerned with, and unaware of, all the uses it is put to. It is the human mind that creates its own difficulties and then cries for help. Is God so partial as to give peace to one person and sorrow to another? In creation there is room for everything, but man refuses to see the good, the healthy and the beautiful, and goes on whining, like the hungry man who sits beside a tasty dish and, instead of stretching out his hand to satisfy his hunger, he goes on lamenting. Whose fault is it, God's or man's? But fortunately for man, God, in His infinite mercy, never forsakes him. He always gives him new chances by providing Gurus and Scriptures to guide him to find the errors of his ways and ultimately gain eternal happiness.

Q. We know that the pleasures of this world are useless and even painful, yet we long for them. What is the way of ending that longing?

M. Think of God and attachments will gradually drop

163

from you. If you wait till all desires disappear to start your devotion and prayer, you will have to wait a very, very long time indeed. [1]

On 4th June 1937 Ramana Maharshi said we only suffer because we identify with the role of the doer.

Q. If God is all, why does the individual suffer for his actions? Are not the actions prompted by Him for which the individual is made to suffer?

M. He who thinks he is the doer is also the sufferer.

Q. But the actions are prompted by God and the individual is only His tool.

M. This logic is applied only when one suffers, but not when one rejoices. If the conviction prevails always, there will be no suffering either.

Q. When will the suffering cease?

M. Not until individuality is lost. If both the good and bad actions are His, why should you think that the enjoyment and suffering are alone yours? He who does good or bad, also enjoys pleasure or suffers pain. Leave it there and do not superimpose suffering on yourself. [2]

On 8th February, 1938 Ramana Maharshi said that right and wrong originate from thoughts and to be free from them you should remain in pure awareness.

Q. What is the best way to work for world peace?

M. What is world? What is peace, and who is the worker?

164

The world is not in your sleep and forms a projection of your mind in your jagrat [waking state]. It is therefore an idea and nothing else. Peace is absence of disturbance. The disturbance is due to the arising of thoughts in the individual, who is only the ego rising up from Pure Consciousness. To bring about peace means to be free from thoughts and to abide as Pure Consciousness. If one remains at peace oneself, there is only peace all about.

Q. If it is a question of doing something one considers wrong, and hereby saving someone else from a great wrong, should one do it or refrain?

M. What is right and wrong? There is no standard by which to judge something to be right and another to be wrong. Opinions differ according to the nature of the individual and according to the surroundings. They are again ideas and nothing more. Do not worry about them. But get rid of thoughts. If you always remain in the right, then right will prevail in the world.[3]

Ramana Maharshi speaks a universal language of a experiencing a 'Oneness with everything' which has echoed down the ages. It is also to be found in Rumi's poem '*A Great Wagon*' which also shows the Absolute, transcending mind and body:

Out beyond ideas
of wrongdoing and rightdoing,
there is a field.
I'll meet you there.

When the soul lies down in that grass,
The world is too full to talk about.
Ideas, language, even the phrase 'each other'
Doesn't make any sense [4]

PART THREE

Thinking or Being

46.

A Life of Thought

Einstein's Legacy

An important part of Einstein's legacy in physics is his use of imaginative conceptual thinking in 'thought experiments'. This extraordinary use of the mind's eye enabled him to formulate revolutionary theories about the laws of nature and the nature of the universe.

For example, when he was 16 years old he imagined himself following a beam of light. They were used in ancient Greece. [1]

Einstein employed a thought experiment to understand his Theory of Special Relativity. He imagined how lightning would appear to a passenger on a moving train compared to an observer on the embankment. If a fork of lightning struck the train tracks simultaneously at two distant points in front of and behind the passenger, an observer on an embankment would see the two bolts of lightning as simultaneous. However, because the passenger is moving towards the bolt of lightning in front of him, he would see this one very slightly earlier than the one behind him.

The lightning strikes are simultaneous with respect to the observer but not with respect to the passenger. This means it cannot be said that the lightning strikes, or any two events are 'absolutely' simultaneous. They are relative to where the observer is.

Einstein's use of thought experiments may also owe something to Spinoza who visualized a flying stone. As we saw earlier, Spinoza believed that if a flying stone had consciousness, it would think that its motion was due to its free will, when in actual fact it was due to external forces.

Einstein was introduced to Spinoza aged 12 by Max Talmey. He soon came to share Spinoza's view of determinism as well as his rejection of the existence of an anthropomorphic God. Years later in Zurich he would study Spinoza's Ethics in the discussion group which he and his young associates dubbed the Olympia Academy

However, as we saw earlier, Einstein was also influenced by Ernst Mach whose work was discussed at the Olympia Academy. Ernst Mach was an Austrin physicist who also allowed his allowed his imagination to roam in the field of physics. [2] According to the Encyclopaedia Britannica "While Mach himself did not explicitly formulate thought experiments, his philosophical stance and critiques provided a foundation for others, like Einstein, to use thought experiments as a tool for exploring and understanding complex scientific concepts."

It may also be significant that when Einstein was a young man, even before the rise to power of the nazis, university careers in experimental physics were barred to Jews who, however, were allowed to pursue careers in theoretical physics. Some scientists had to literally imagine their experiments!

Einstein's use of imaginative conceptual thinking 'thought experiments' may well have been introduced to him and encouraged by Max Talmey and further developed by discussions about Spinoza and Ernst Mach in the Olympia Academy.

Einstein was dedicated to perceiving and understanding reality by his imaginative thought processes. He would then validate his theories with mathematics. He did not like anything which interfered with his thinking and he freed himself from personal relationships, preferring solitude so that he could spend almost all his time in thought. This was highlighted by the English psychiatrist Anthony Storr:

"The most remarkable thing about Einstein's achievement is that his discoveries were made almost entirely by thought alone, unsupported at first by experiment or indeed by much mathematics. The paper on the special theory of relativity, published in 1905, contains no references, very little mathematics and quotes no authority. Indeed his knowledge of mathematics was, at that time, sketchy compared with that of other leading physicists." [3]

Einstein did not want to be emotionally involved with anyone or be influenced in any way. His biographer, Antonia Vallentin, who knew Einstein and his second wife, wrote:

"His social conscience seems almost detached from its object. He has never really needed human contact but has deliberately freed himself more and more from all emotional dependence in order to become entirely self-sufficient. Real intimacy and the unconditional sharing of thoughts and feelings with another person, so that they become almost another self, is an experience he has hardly ever had: he fears it because it threatens the complete inner freedom which his essential to him." [4]

Einstein kept his life simple and avoided complexities. This almost certainly helped him to use his thinking to imagine some of the forces behind the laws of nature. His mind, clear of other thoughts, was also able to see its own limitations.

Although Einstein, communicated his thoughts through many papers, books letters and lectures, like Ramana Maharshi, he was clearly aware of the limits of thinking.

He left a vast amount of written material which is still being translated, transcribed and annotated by the *Einstein Archive* and many other sources in the form of the numerous volumes of the *Collected Papers of Albert Einstein*. These are now available digitally. [5]

But perhaps Einstein's greatest legacy is his second one which comes from all of his conclusions. As a result of his conclusions about the secrets of nature in understanding the universe, Einstein was able to describe his understanding of God.

"Try and penetrate with our limited means the secrets of nature and you will find that, behind all the discernible laws and connections, there remains something subtle, intangible, and inexplicable. Veneration for this force beyond anything that we can comprehend is my religion. To that extent I am, in point of fact, religious." [6]

Einstein was in awe of what it was possible to see and he had reverential respect for it. Awareness of his inability to understand it produced a feeling of humility.

And perhaps his third legacy was his concern with morality. He was active in trying to prevent the deterioration of morality at a time when it was dominated by organised religions. He thought morality should not be based on any religion. He believed religious teachers should give up the idea of a personal God which is the source of fear and hope which gives priests vast amounts of power.

Einstein was at the cutting edge of new scientific ideas which are still emerging and being developed from his original insights. His search for a unified field theory was in vain. He did not seek an equation for the relationship between technology and humanity but could it be that as one goes up the other tends to come down? Einstein's life spanned both the development of the atomic bomb and the industrialized slaughter of the Holocaust. Could it be that our use of technology risks being inversely proportional to our realisation as civilised human beings?

47.

A Life of Being Still

Ramana Maharshi's Legacy

Most of the time Ramana Maharshi did not communicate by talking. Instead, he communicated his teaching through silence and being still. The little he wrote amounts to only a few thousand words, *The Collected works of Ramana Maharshi.* [1]

As we saw earlier, the written recorded dialogues over three years in the book, 'Talks with Sri Ramana Maharshi,' show that he spoke on only 220 out of 1095 days; roughly, on average, once every five days which by any standard is virtual silence. When he did speak, it was only to pass his teaching on to those who did not understand his silent teaching, which he regarded as more direct. When he answered questions, he often spoke in terms of the religion of the particular questioner, which was mostly Hindu or Christian.

Despite the existence of written transcriptions of his words and numerous books about him, his silent teaching continues to be considered a major part of his legacy today.

Although it may seem counterintuitive to teach in silence, what he was teaching was inner stillness. Words engender words. Sri Ramana's silence engendered silence, that is the peace of having transcended thought. Is there any better way to teach not having thoughts than by not thinking, not speaking and just being an example of having transcended thought? His teaching is beyond thought because it is Awareness. It transcends thought.

In his realised state of stillness Ramana Maharshi was clearly a quiet person but he was not inactive. He answered visitor's questions, took daily walks on Arunachala and was frequently involved preparing food in the kitchen. He read correspondence as well as newspapers and took an interest in the details of many people's lives.

Unlike Einstein, Ramana Maharshi's view was that morality was based on ideas only and they varied depending on the nature of the person and their environment. He said it was the responsibility of the individual to get rid of thoughts and to remain in the right, then right would prevail in the world.

Much of his legacy is contained in what he said about peace and it is worth repeating because it is fundamental to the way he lived and taught.

On 8th February, 1938 Ramana Maharshi said that right and wrong originate from thoughts and to be free from them you should remain in pure awareness.

Q. What is the best way to work for world peace?

M. What is world? What is peace, and who is the worker? The world is not in your sleep and forms a projection of your mind in your jagrat [waking state]. It is therefore an idea and nothing else. Peace is absence of disturbance. The disturbance is due to the arising of thoughts in the individual, who is only the ego rising up from Pure Consciousness. To bring about peace means to be free from thoughts and to abide as Pure Consciousness. If one remains at peace oneself, there is only peace all about.

Q. If it is a question of doing something one considers wrong, and hereby saving someone else from a great wrong, should one do it or refrain?

M. What is right and wrong? There is no standard by which to judge something to be right and another to be wrong.

Opinions differ according to the nature of the individual and according to the surroundings. They are again ideas and nothing more. Do not worry about them. But get rid of thoughts. If you always remain in the right, then right will prevail in the world.[2]

48.

Compassion

Both Einstein and Ramana Maharshi were men of considerable compassion. They understood in remarkable depth the difficulty people have with understanding our false sense of separateness. But they had completely different ways of communicating this.

Einstein's showed his compassion for the rabbi who lost his son by bringing to bear his knowledge of religion and philosophy in writing to provide a way to deal with his grief. He advised him that to find peace of mind he needed to overcome his delusion of separateness. That is to find inside a oneness with everything.

Ramana Maharshi's compassion was demonstrated when a woman who had lost her husband to a shark whilst he was swimming in the sea, came to see him with a long list of questions. As recalled by Katya Osborne: [1]

'When asked what he said to her she answered "Nothing." She had her list of questions which she took out. When he looked at her, he looked so compassionate, she suddenly thought, "It doesn't matter." '

Somehow, through Ramana Maharshi's presence and 'look' she had found the peace of mind Einstein had advised the rabbi to find by removing his delusion of separateness. This woman's altered awareness had enabled her to transcend her grief which up until then had been insurmountable.

Here the crucial difference between Einstein and Ramana Maharshi is that whilst Einstein was aware of the consequences of our delusion of separateness and described it in writing, Ramana Maharshi was able to show ways to end our separateness, and how to accomplish it.

Ramana Maharshi was frequently visited by animals living around him. These included dogs, monkeys, squirrels, cows and peacocks. He had great respect for their intelligence and was full of compassion for them. He said that they may be working out the same things about this world as we are. Birds and squirrels used to build their nests around him. [2]

He showed them the same respect as he showed to humans. For example, it was a rule that at mealtimes the animals were always fed before anyone else. He showed compassion for animals when they were upset or unwell. On their leaving the body, they were buried with the same respect given to humans. When his favourite cow, Lakshmi, was dying, he sat beside her for nearly an hour.

"He sat down beside her and took her head on his lap. He gazed into her eyes and placed his hand on her head as though giving her diksha [initiation] and also over her heart. Holding his cheek against hers, he caressed her." [3] [4]

Until the last few years monkeys still came to the window beside Sri Bhagavan's couch and looked in through the bars. Sometimes one saw monkey mothers with the little ones clinging to them, as if to show them to Bhagavan, just as human mothers did. [5]

Raman Maharshi had equal respect for animals as humans and once said:

"We do not know what souls may be tenanting these bodies and for finishing what part of their unfinished karma they may seek our company." [6]

It seems Ramana Maharshi knew he was not separate from anything including animals and lived his life being one with everything.

The lens through which Ramana Maharshi perceived and

understood the world was through 'awareness of oneness with everything,' by transcending thinking and not using words.

Einstein, like Ramana Maharshi, led as much as was possible a simple life in America. He spent much of his time in solitude using his thinking to try to come up with an answer to what turned out to be the unfathomable.

Ramana Maharshi arrived at Arunachala in 1896 aged 16 and remained in silence for the first 11 years, occasionally writing answers to visitors' questions.

From 1907 onwards, he maintained virtual silence only speaking to answer questions asked by visitors who did not understand his silent teaching

Ramana Maharshi was often surrounded by people who wanted to be in his presence so that they too could uncover and recognise their own 'awareness of oneness with everything,' and be at peace being still.

49

The End

Einstein died in Princeton Hospital, apparently still searching for an answer for his Unified Field Theory. He was alone at night when he uttered his last words in German which were heard by a nurse attending him who did not understand German.

A scrap of paper with a complex handwritten equation he had just been working on, was found beside him on his bed. It seems the one thing he was aware of at the time of his death was his concept of God.

Ramana Maharshi died in a small room in his ashram on the lower slopes of Arunachala surrounded by his attendants and devotees.

Some of the devotees made a plea for their own welfare when they said:

"What is to become of us without Bhagavan? We are too weak to look after ourselves; we depend on his Grace for everything." And he replied:

"You attach too much importance to the body," clearly implying that the end of his body would not interrupt the Grace and guidance. In the same vein he said:

"They say that I am dying but I am not going away. Where could I go? I am here."[1]

Coming from almost opposite viewpoints at around the same time, Albert Einstein and Ramana Maharshi explored our nature using imaginative conceptual thinking and pure awareness.

Much of Einstein's and Ramana Maharshi's influence on us is only now being understood. Their understanding, wisdom and compassion are becoming an important point of reference for us in our highly technical and increasingly impersonal world.

50.

Epilogue

A visitor's experience of Ramana Maharshi

I first met Narikutti Swami on Arunachala in 1985 because the airline which took me to India lost my luggage and I needed some clothes. I was introduced to him by Chris Quilkey who said Narikutti would take me to a tailor to get some clothes made as I only had what I was wearing.

Narikutti Swami (Barry Windsor) was born in 1930 in Sydney where he was an architect. He worked with some of Sydney's best architects including Peter Muller and Adrian Snodgrass. He travelled with Adrian Snodgrass to Sri Lanka in 1957. [1]

During our many subsequent meetings over the next ten years we usually discussed things walking around Arunachala or in chai shops over coffee.

Narikutti told me about his time in Sri Lanka with Yoga Swami of Jaffna. He also mentioned some of Yoga Swami's other followers whom he spent time with when he was living in Sri Lanka. They included: Santha Swami (James Ramsbotham, who was later to be known as Viscount Lord Soulbury) who wrote about Yoga Swami [2] and the Architect Adrian Snodgrass. [3]

Most importantly, he also told me about Yoga Swami's meeting with Ramana Maharshi in the 1930's. Yoga Swami of Jaffna was Sri Lanka's best known 20th century Sage.

Narikutti Swami was a follower of Yoga Swami of Jaffna from 1957 until Yoga Swami died in 1964. [4] In 1970 Narikutti Swami moved to Tiruvannamalai to live on Arunachala, which he helped reforest. He died there in 1994.

Narikutti Swami said that in the 1930's Yoga Swami visited Ramana Maharshi in his ashram in Tiruvannamalai and they sat opposite each other one afternoon for over an hour. During this time they sat in silence, neither of them saying a word.

When he returned to Sri Lanka Yoga Swami remarked: "We said all that had to be said."

Yoga Swami, who never overtly praised anyone, called Ramana Maharshi a "maha viran", a "great hero". [5]

Yogaswami is known for his four aphorisms:

We do not know

All is truth

There is not even one thing wrong

It was all accomplished long ago [6]

Yoga Swami

Glossary

Abhyasi	Aspirant
Aham Brahmasmi	I am the ultimate reality, I am Brahman
Ahankar	'I' sense; the ego-self
Antahkarana	Total mind
Arunachala	A hill in Tiruvannamalai district, Tamil Nadu, South India
Atma	The Self or Soul
Atma-vichara	Self-enquiry
Atmic	The highest consciousness, the Self, Soul
Awareness	Knowledge of something which is concentrating attention on one thought, subjective, transcendent and beyond words
Bar mitzvah	A Jewish ceremony marking a boy's transition at 13 years old from a boy to a man and living according to Jewish law
Bhagavan	A term of respect meaning 'Lord'
Bhakti-marga	Path of devotion
Brahmachari	The first of four stages in life in Hinduism: brahmacharya, grihastha, vanaprastha, and sannyasa
Bhagavan	A title of veneration often meaning 'Lord'
Bhuminatheswara Temple	A Siva temple where Venkataraman (Ramana Maharshi's childhood name) used to play and seek refuge
Brahman	The ultimate universal reality, the cause of everything that exists uniting everything including consciousness as a single binding unity

Buddhi	Intellect
Consciousness	Ability to process information, open to attend to streams of thought, can be discussed and categorised
Dhyana	Meditation/concentration
Diksha	Initiation
Doership	Having the feeling we are the doer, when it is directed by cosmic law
Evans-Wentz	American anthropologist, and early translator of The Tibetan Book of the Dead
Gayatri	A well known Vedic mantra
Hiranyagarbha	Universal consciousness
'I-I'	The infinite I, not associated with the body and senses
Ishta devata	A worshipper's favourite deity
Isvaro gururatmeti	God is the same as Guru and Self
Jagrat	The waking state
Japa	Mantra
Jnana marga	Knowledge of the Self, wisdom
Karam	Doing something
karma	Three main types: Sanchita: accumulated karma of former births. Prarabdha: That part of one's karma which is to be worked out in this life. Agami: actions expected to bear fruit in future births.
kirtam	Narrating or describing
koshas	Layers of being

Isvara:, Isvara,	The Supreme Being in His aspect as the Lord of all creation
Mahatma	Enlightened person
Maha viran	A great hero
Maharshi	Great Sage
Manas	The human processing mind
Marga	Path
Maya	Illusion
Moksha	Liberation, spiritual freedom
Nasrudin	A character in the folklore of the Muslim world
Nostra Culpa	Through our own fault
Panentheistic	Seeing God as greater than the universe, than all things, beyond space and time
Panpsychism	The Theory that consciousness is the fundamental feature of reality which exists throughout the universe.
Pantheistic	Seeing God in all things, that everything in the universe is God
Peria Puranam	A 12th century poetic Tamil account of sixty-three saints
Pradakshina	The 8 ½ mile (14 kms) walk around Arunachala
Prana	Life Force
Pranayama	Method of breathing
Prarabdha:	That part of one's karma which is to be worked out in this life

Predeterminism	The philosophy that all events of history, past, present and future, have been already decided or are already known (by God, fate, or some other force), including human actions.
Realisation	Awakening to how we are
Sadhana	Spiritual practice
Sakshat	With one's own eyes
Sakshatkaram	Direct perception of the Self
Samadhi	The state of directly experiencing the Self, blissful meditative awareness
Samskara	Latent tendencies
Sarangati	Devotion. Complete surrender to God
Self Enquiry	Self knowledge
Sankaracharya	(Adi Shankara) an Indian Vedic scholar, and teacher of Advaita Vedanta.
Siva	The Self or one of the three main Hindu deities
Sri	Resplendent, dazzling
Thought experiments	Using the imagination to conceptualise the results of experiments which are not possible to practically perform.
Tiruchuli	The birthplace of Ramana Maharshi A town in Tamil Nadu 45 km south of Madurai,
Tiruvannamalai	A temple town in Tamil Nadu enclosing the Temple and the Hill Arunachala
Transcend	To go beyond the limits, to rise above, especially thought

Transpersonal psychology	An umbrella term for a branch of psychology which includes looking at transcendent experiences as well as awareness of the human spirit.
Vedanta	Philosophy from the Upanishadic texts
Vichara	Self-enquiry
Yogananda	An Indian monk who helped introduce yoga and meditation. Author of Autobiography of a Yogi

References

CHAPTER 1   Opposite sides of the Same Coin

1. Jung, C. G. *The Collected Works of C.G. Jung.* Vol 11
    Princeton: Princeton: Princeton University Press (1969) p.577

CHAPTER 2   The First Awakening - Max Talmey

1. Jammer, Max, *Einstein and Religion,* Princeton (1999) p. 24-25

2. Schilpp, Paul Arthur, (Ed.) 'Autobiographical Notes' in
    *Albert Einstein: Philosopher- Scientist, T*he Library of Living
    Philosophers Volume VII p. 3-5, available at https://www. amazon.
    co.uk/Albert-Einstein-Philosopher-Scientist-Library-Philosophers/
    dp/0875482864?asin=0875482864&revisionId=&format=4&depth=1
    accessed on 16 January 01 2025

CHAPTER 3   The Second Awakening - School

1. Einstein, Albert, *The Collected Papers of Albert Einstein, The Early Years,*
    1879-1902 (English Translation Supplement) Page xxi (21 of 220),
    Princeton University Press and the Hebrew University, available
    at https://einsteinpapers.press.princeton.edu/vol1-trans/21?
    highlightText=nervous+breakdown, accessed 16 January 2025

2. Storr, Anthony, *The Dynamics of Creation*, Pelican, (1972) p.93

3. Einstein, Albert, *The Collected Papers of Albert Einstein, The Early Years,*
    1879-1902 (English Translation Supplement) Page xxi (21 of 220),
    Princeton University Press and the Hebrew University, available
    at https://einsteinpapers.press.princeton.edu/vol1-trans/21?
    highlightText=nervous+breakdown, accessed 16 January 2025

4. Obituary, *Anthony Storr*, Cambridge University Press, available at https://www.cambridge.org/core/services/aop-cambridge-core/content/view/D3340401EBA15790759A83D498 D6A0A7/S0955603600023072a.pdf/anthony-storr.pdf, accessed 16 January 2025

5. Wikipedia, *Winchester College*, available at https://en.wikipedia.org/wiki/Winchester_College, accessed 16 January 2025

6. Wikipedia, *Makin Review*, available at https://en.wikipedia.org/wiki/Makin_Review, accessed 16 January 2025

7. Sherwood, Harriet, (18 January 2022). *"Winchester college society was cult-like, finds report into child abuse"*. The Guardian, available at https://www.theguardian.com/education/2022/jan/18/winchester-college-christian-forum-society-report-child-abuse, accessed 28 January 2025

8. John Smyth, QC *"Review of Abuse in The 1970s and 1980s of Pupils from Winchester College,"*available at https://www.winchestercollege.org/stories/a-statement-from-the-warden-and-fellows-of-winchester-college, accessed at 28 January 2025

9. Isaacson, Walter, *Einstein, His Life and Universe.* Simon & Schuster UK Ltd (2007) p. 22

10. Maja Einstein, xx; Seelig 1956a, 15; Pais 1982, 38; Einstein draft to Philipp Frank, 1940, CPAE 1, p. lxiii.

11. Einstein, Albert, *The Collected Papers of Albert Einstein, The Early Years*, 1879-1902 (English Translation Supplement) Page xxi (21 of 220), Princeton University Press and the Hebrew University, available at https://einsteinpapers.press.princeton.edu/vol1-trans/21?highlightText=nervous+breakdown, accessed 16 January 2025

CHAPTER 4 The Third Awakening - The Olympia Academy

1. Highfield J. R. L.,*The Private Lives of Albert Einstein* Faber & Faber (1994) p.97-97 available at https://archive.org/detailsprivatelivesofa l00high_1/page/96/mode/2up,accessed 16 January 2025

2. Books discussed *Olympia Academy* available at org/wiki/ Olympia_Academy accessed 16 January 2025

3. *Einstein's Thought Experiments,* available at https://en.wikipedia .org/wiki/Einstein%27s_thought_experiments, accessed 16 January 2025

4. Caltech, *Einstein Papers Project, The Collected Papers of Albert Einstein.* Einstein and Mach: Creating History and Philosophy of Physics as a Discipline, available at https://www.einstein.caltech.edu/news/ einstein-and-mach-creating-history-and-philosophy-of-physics- as-a-discipline#:~:text=Mach%20sided%20with%20Leibniz%20 against,was%20also%20a%20relative%20matter, accessed 16 January 2025

5. Highfield J. R. L., *The Private Lives of Albert Einstein* Faber & Faber (1994) p.97-97, available at https://archive.org/details/ privatelivesofal0000high/page/96/mode/2up, accessed 8 March 2025

CHAPTER 5 Disbelief in Free Will

1. From an interview with G.S. Viereck, " *What life Means to Einstein"* Saturday Evening Post, October 26, 1929; reprinted in Viereck, Glimpses of the Great Duckworth London p.367-376 (1930), available at https://archive.org/details/dli.ernet.13528/ page/369/mode/2up, accessed 16 January 2025

2. Saturday Evening Post, 'What life Means to Einstein,' (1929), available at https://www.saturdayeveningpost.com/wp-content/ uploads/satevepost/what_life_means_to_einstein.pdf, accessed 22 February 2025

3. Ibid.

4. Mudaliar, Devaraja, *Day by Day with Bhagavan.* Sri Ramanasramam (2013) p. 266

CHAPTER 6 Knowing and Believing

1. New York Times April 25, 1929

2. BBC, John Freeman interview, *'Face to Face with Carl Jung,'* BBC 1959, available at https://www.bbc.co.uk/iplayer/episode/p04q hvyj/face-to-face-carl-jung, accessed 16 January 2025

CHAPTER 7 The Harmonious Force Behind Nature

1. Hoffmann, Banesh. *Letter to Professor Marvin Magalaner* April 26 1947 in *Albert Einstein : Creator and Rebel* (1973)

2. New York Times *Albert Einstein Obituary,* April 19, 1955. Dukas and Hoffman, *Albert Einstein The Human Side-Glimpses from His Archives* p. 66 (1979)

3. Venkataramiah, Munagala, S, *Talks with Sri Ramana Maharshi,* Sri Ramanasramam. (2013) Talk 502 p. 499-500)

4. From *"What I believe,"* Forum and Century 84 (1930), available at https://opensiddur.org/prayers/solilunar/everyday/daytime/ addenda/wie-ich-die-welt-sehe-what-i-believe-an-essay-by- albert-einstein-1930-1934/, accessed 28 January 2025

5. Plank, Max, *"Das Wesen der Materie"* (*The Nature of Matter*), speech at Florence, Italy (1944) (from Archiv zur Geschichte der Max-Planck-Gesellschaft, Abt. Va, Rep. 11 Planck, Nr. 1797), available at https://en.wikiquote.org/wiki/Max_Planck, accessed 28 January 2025

CHAPTER 8 Acknowledging being a Religious Person

1. Kessler, Harry. Dinner conversation between Alfred Kerr and Einstein recorded in, *The Diary of a Cosmopolitan* (1971)June 14, 1927.

2. From *"What I believe,"* Forum and Century 84 (1930), available at https://opensiddur.org/prayers/solilunar/everyday/daytime/addenda/wie-ich-die-welt-sehe-what-i-believe-an-essay-by-albert-einstein-1930-1934/, accessed 16 January 2025

3. Dukas and Hoffman, *Albert Einstein The Human Side-Glimpses from His Archives* Princeton (1979) p. 39

CHAPTER 9 Levels of Attainment

1. New York Times Magazine on November 9, 1930 pp 1-4. Reprinted in *Ideas and Opinions*, Crown Publishers, Inc. 1954, pp 36 - 40. It appears in Albert Einstein, *The World as I See It*, Philosophical Library, New York, 1949, pp. 24 - 28, available at https://namnews.wordpress.com/wp-content/uploads/2012/04/29289146-ideas-and-opinions-by-albert-einstein.pdf, accessed 16 January 2025

2. Venkataramiah, Munagala, S, *Talks with Sri Ramana Maharshi*, Sri Ramanasramam. (2013) Talk 595 p. 567

3. New York Times Magazine on November 9, 1930 pp 1-4. Reprinted in *Ideas and Opinions*, Crown Publishers, Inc. 1954, pp 36 - 40. It appears in Albert Einstein, *The World as I See It*, Philosophical Library, New York, 1949, pp. 24 - 28, available at https://namnews.wordpress.com/wp-content/uploads/2012/04/29289146-ideas-and-opinions-by-albert-einstein.pdf, accessed 16 January 2025

4. Venkataramiah, Munagala, S, *Talks with Sri Ramana Maharshi*, Sri Ramanasramam. (2013) Talks 596 p. 568

5. New York Times Magazine on November 9, 1930 pp 1-4. Reprinted in I*deas and Opinions*, Crown Publishers, Inc. 1954, pp 36 - 40. It appears in Albert Einstein, *The World as I See It*, Philosophical Library, New York, 1949, pp. 24 - 28, available at https://namnews.wordpress.com/wp-content/uploads/2012/04/29289146-ideas-and-opinions-by-albert-einstein.pdf, accessed 16 January 2025

6. Venkataramiah, Munagala, S, *Talks with Sri Ramana Maharshi,* Sri Ramanasramam. (2013) Talk 595 p. 568

7. Ibid., Talk 502 p. 499-500

CHAPTER 10 Realising Our Inner Nature

1. Venkataramiah, Munagala, S, *Talks with Sri Ramana Maharshi,* Sri Ramanasramam. (2013) Talks 523 p. 522

2. New York Times Magazine on November 9, 1930 pp 1-4. Reprinted in I*deas and Opinions,* Crown Publishers, Inc. 1954, pp 36 - 40. It appears in Albert Einstein, *The World as I See It,* Philosophical Library, New York, 1949, pp. 24 - 28, available at https://namnews.wordpress.com/wp-content/uploads/2012/04/29289146-ideas-and-opinions-by-albert-einstein.pdf, accessed 16 January 2025, accessed 16 January 2025

CHAPTER 11   Separating Morality from Organised Religion

1. New York Times Magazine on November 9, 1930 pp 1-4. Reprinted in *Ideas and Opinions,* Crown Publishers, Inc. 1954, pp 36 - 40. It appears in Albert Einstein, *The World as I See It,* Philosophical Library, New York, 1949, pp. 24 - 28, available at https://namnews.wordpress.com/wp-content/uploads/2012/04/29289146-ideas-and-opinions-by-albert-einstein.pdf, accessed 16 January 2025

2. Excerpt from *Science, Philosophy and Religion, A Symposium,* published by the Conference on Science, Philosophy and Religion in Their Relation to the Democratic Way of Life, Inc., New York, 1941. Available at https://sacred-texts.com/aor/einstein/einsci.htm, accessed 16 January 2025

3. Ibid.

4. Dukas and Hoffman, *Albert Einstein The Human Side-Glimpses from His Archives* p. (1979) Princeton p. 94

5. Dukas and Hoffman, *Albert Einstein The Human Side-Glimpses from His Archives* p. (1979) Princeton p. 95

6. Nimenko, W, *Uncovering and Recognising Awareness* Goalpath books (2024) p.34

CHAPTER 12 Morality is more Crucial than Science and Technology

1. Dukas and Hoffman, *Albert Einstein The Human Side-Glimpses from His Archives,* Princeton (1979) p.70

CHAPTER 13 The Dehumanising Impact of Technology

1. Dukas and Hoffman, *Albert Einstein The Human Side-Glimpses from His Archives* Princeton (1979)p.82

2. Nimenko W. (2018) *Virtual Reality and Sacred Places.* The Mountain Path, (2018) Vol 55 No, 4, Sri Ramanasramam

CHAPTER 14 Intellectual Destruction of Human Relationships.

1. Einstein, Albert. *"The Need for Ethical Culture"* in Mein Weltbild; *Ideas and Opinions*, p 53-54, available at https://nam news.wordpress.com/wp-content/uploads/2012/04/29289146-ideas-and-opinions-by-albert-einstein.pdf, accessed 16 January 2025

2. Kropotkin, Peter, (1902). *Mutual Aid: A Factor of Evolution.* McClure, Philips & Company

3. BBC, *In Our Time, Peter Kropotkin,* available at https://www.bbc.co.uk/programmes/m0014pfr, accessed 16 January, 2025

CHAPTER 15 Limitations of the Intellect, Psychology and Analysis

1. Letter to S. Ferenczi, 2nd January 1927 *The Collected Papers of Sigmund Freud*, ed. Ernest Jones.

2. Dukas and Hoffman, *Albert Einstein The Human Side-Glimpses from His Archives*, Princeton, (1979) p. 35

3. From and interview with G.S. Viereck, " *What life Means to Einstein*" Saturday Evening Post, October 26, 1929; reprinted in Viereck, Glimpses of the Great Duckworth London p.367-376 (1930), available at https://archive.org/details/dli.ernet.13528/page/369/mode/2up, accessed 16 January 2025

4. Saturday Evening Post, 'What life Means to Einstein,' (1929), available at https://www.saturdayeveningpost.com/wp-content/uploads/satevepost/what_life_means_to_einstein.pdf, accessed 22 February 2025

5. Diary entry December 6, 1931. See Nathan and Norden, *Einstein on Peace,* 1931.3, available at https://archive.org/details/dli.ernet.13528/page/369/mode/2up,accessed 16 January 2025

6. Storr, A. *Feet of Clay. A study of Gurus* (Harper Collins Publishers, 1996), p 91

7. Ibid p 96

CHAPTER 16 Path of the Choiceless

1. League of Nations (1933) *Why War? Freud and Einstein's correspondence,* available at https://www.sas.upenn.edu/~cavitch/pdf-library/Freud_and_Einstein_Why_War.pdf, accessed 16 January 2025

2. *Letters of Sigmund Freud,* ed. Ernst L. Freud (New York: Basic Books, 1960. Einstein Archives 32-567

CHAPTER 17 Einstein's Impact on Psychology

1. Jung, C.G. *Letters of C. G. Jung*: Princeton University Press;
   Reissue edition (1 July 1992) Volume 2, 1951-1961 p 108-109,
   available at https://www.reddit.com/r/Jung/comments/1atkux6/
   jung_in_genius_einsteins_life_based_on_the_book/, accessed
   5 February 2025

2. Webster, Richard, *Why Freud was Wrong*. Orwell Press
   (1995), available at   https://www.karnacbooks.com/product/
   why-freud-was-wrong-sin-science-and-psychoanalysis/503/,
   accessed 28 January 2025

3. Storr, A. *Feet of Clay. A Study of Gurus* (Harper Collins Publishers,
   1996), p 91-97

4. Viktor Frankl, *Mans Search For Meaning*, available at
   file:///F:/S%20DISC%20%2015%2012%202024/1.%20Wasyl%2018
   %2011%202024/12.%20Spiritual%2004%2002%202024/Viktor
   Frankl_Mans%20Search.pdf, accessed 16 January 2025

5. Gordon-Brown, I. with Somers Barbara. *The Raincloud of Knowable
   Things*. (Archive Publishing, (2008)

6. Nimenko, W, *Do you need a Doctor, Therapist or Guru?*, Goalpath
   books (2023)

7. Wikipedia, available at https://en.wikipedia.org/wiki/Synchronicity
   accessed on 5 February 2025

8. Dukas and Hoffman, *Albert Einstein The Human Side-Glimpses
   from His Archives*, Princeton (1979) p.70

9. Jung, C. G. *The Collected Works of C.G. Jung,* Vol 11 (Princeton:
   Princeton University Press 1969), p.584

CHAPTER 18 Losing Our Way then Remembering Einstein

1. Dawson, Lorne L. *Cults and New Religious Movements: A Reader* (Blackwell Readings in Religion). Blackwell Publishing (2003). Professional. P. 54.

2. Dukas and Hoffman, *Albert Einstein The Human Side-Glimpses from His Archives,* Princeton (1979) p.70

CHAPTER 19 The Bliss of No Want

1. From and interview with G.S. Viereck, " *What life Means to Einstein"* Saturday Evening Post, October 26, 1929; reprinted in Viereck, Glimpses of the Great Duckworth London p.367-376 (1930), available at https://archive.org/details/dli.ernet.13528/page/369/mode/2up, accessed 16 January 2025

2. Saturday Evening Post, 'What life Means to Einstein,' (1929), available at https://www.saturdayeveningpost.com/wp-content/uploads/satevepost/what_life_means_to_einstein.pdf, accessed 22 February 2025

3. Venkataramiah, Munagala, S, *Talks with Sri Ramana Maharshi,* Sri Ramanasramam. (2013) Talks 648 p. 628

4. From *"What I believe,"* Forum and Century 84 (1930), available at https://opensiddur.org/prayers/solilunar/everyday/daytime/addenda/wie-ich-die-welt-sehe-what-i-believe-an-essay-by-albert-einstein-1930-1934/, accessed 16 January 2025

5. Narasimha Swami B.V, Ch. XXII *Self Realisation* (1937) p. 142-146

CHAPTER 20 Proving what Science Denies

1. Dukas and Hoffman, *Albert Einstein The Human Side-Glimpses from His Archives* Princeton (1979)p.32-33

2. Shah, Idries, *The Elephant in the Dark,* Octagon Press (1974]

3. Wikipedia, *Blind men and an elephant*, available at https://en.wikip ediA.org/wiki/Blind_men_and_an_elephant, accessed 16 January 2025

4. Shah, Idries, *"The Teaching Story: Observations on the Folklore of Our "Modern" Thought"*. Archived from the original on 2011-07-18. Retrieved 2010-03-05.

CHAPTER 21 Einstein and Brahman.

1. Modern Review *On the Nature of Reality.* The Recorded discussion between Albert Einstein and Rabindranath Tagore at Caputh, near Berlin, on July 14, 1930. Published January, 1931, available at https://mast.queensu.ca/~murty/einstein_tagore.pdf accessed 16 January 2025

2. Naive Realism, available at https://en.wikipedia.org/wiki/ Na%C3%AFve_realism, accessed 20 February 2025

3. Transcendental Realism, available at https://en.wikipedia.org/wiki/ Transcendental_idealism, accessed 20 February 2025

4. Plank, Max, *Max Plank Interview* in 'The Observer' (25 January 1931), p.17, column 3, available at https://www.newspapers.com/article/ the-observer-max-planck-observer-12531/25590070/?locale=en-GB, accessed 16 January 2025

5. Panpsychism Wikipedia, available at https://en.wikipedia.org/wiki/ Panpsychism accessed 18 February 2025

6. Nimenko, Wasyl, *Searching in Secret New Zealand and Australia,* Goalpath Books ((2016) p. 74-76

7. Brunton, Paul, *'A Search in Secret India.'* Rider (1934)

8. Venkataramiah, Munagala, S, *Talks with Sri Ramana Maharshi,* Sri Ramanasramam. (2013) Talks 446. p. 431-432

CHAPTER 22 Truth

1. Shah, Idries, *The Exploits of the Incomparable Mulla Nasrudin*
   Jonathan Cape (1966)

2. Spinoza, Baruch, *Tractatus Theologicae-Philosophicus*
   Everyman edition. The Modern Library, (1927) p. 34

CHAPTER 23 Essence of Awareness

1. Jung, C. G. *The Collected Works of C.G. Jung.* Vol 11
   Princeton: Princeton: Princeton University Press 1969) p.577

CHAPTER 24 Awakening

1. Sri Ramanasramam, *The Collected Works of Ramana Maharshi,*
   (2001) p. 96

2. Osborne, A. *Ramana Maharshi and the Path of Self-Knowledge.*
   Sri Ramanasramam (2002) p. 8-10

3. Mudaliar, Devaraja, *Day by Day with Bhagavan.* Sri Ramanasramam
   (2013) p. 47-48)

CHAPTER 25 Arunachala

1. Greenblatt, Joan, Greenblatt, Matthew. *Bhagavan Sri Ramana*
   A Pictorial Biography, Sri Ramanasramam (1981) p. 10

2. Sri Ramanasramam, *The Collected Works of Ramana Maharshi,*
   (2001) p. 82

3. Sri Ramanasramam, *The Collected Works of Ramana Maharshi,*
   (2001) p. 85

4. Sri Ramanasramam, *The Collected Works of Ramana Maharshi,*
   (2001) p. 104-107

CHAPTER 26 Levels of Attainment

1. Venkataramiah, Munagala, S, *Talks with Sri Ramana Maharshi,*
   Sri Ramanasramam. (2013) Talks 595 p. 567

2. Ibid., Talks 596 p. 567-569

CHAPTER 27 The Eloquence of Silence

1. Gattegno, Caleb, *Silent Way,* Educational Solutions, Inc.,(1963)

2. Venkataramiah, Munagala, S. *Talks with Sri Ramana Maharshi*,
   Sri Ramanasramam. (2013) Talks 20 p. 18

3. Ibid., *Talks* 246, p. 209

4. Katya Douglas, *Kitty Osborne's Memories of Bhagavan Sri Ramana
   Maharshi*, available at https://www.youtube.com/
   watch?v=Q4K5IzjJK-k, accessed 12 February 2025

5. Venkataramiah, Munagala, S, *Talks with Sri Ramana Maharshi*,
   Sri Ramanasramam. (2013) Talks 394 p. 377

6. Ibid., *Talks* 599 p. 573

CHAPTER 28 Silently Still

1. Venkataramiah, Munagala. S, *Talks with Sri Ramana Maharshi,*
   Sri Ramanasramam. (2013)

2. Nagamma, Suri, *Letters from Sri Ramanasramam,*
   Sri Ramanasramam (1985)

3. Mudaliar, Devaraja, *Day by Day with Bhagavan.* Sri Ramanasramam
   (2013) p. 265

CHAPTER 29   Discernment

1. Venkataramiah, Munagala, S, *Talks with Sri Ramana Maharshi,* Sri Ramanasramam. (2013) Talks 141 p. 126

2. Ibid., *Talks* 41 p. 47

3. Ibid., *Talks* 198 p.170

CHAPTER 30   The Bliss of No Want

1. Venkataramiah, Munagala, S, *Talks with Sri Ramana Maharshi,* Sri Ramanasramam. (2013) Talks 3 p. 1

2. Sri Ramanasramam (2002) *Who AM I?* in *The Collected Works of Ramana Maharshi,* (2001) 24

3. Venkataramiah, Munagala, S, *Talks with Sri Ramana Maharshi,* Sri Ramanasramam (2013) Talks 648 p. 628

CHAPTER 31   The Wound's Gift

1. Cohen, Leonard, *Anthem* in *The Future,* Columbia records (1992)

2. Calaprice, Alice, *Dear Professor Einstein: Albert Einstein's Letters to and from Children.* Foreword by Evelyn Einstein. Amherst, N.Y.: Prometheus, 2002.

3. Ibid.

CHAPTER 32   Loss of a Child

1. Venkataramiah, Munagala, S, *Talks with Sri Ramana Maharshi,* Sri Ramanasramam. (2013) Talks 80 p. 83

2. Ibid., *Talks* 251 p. 215

3. Ibid., *Talks* 276 p. 242-243

4. Jung, C. G., *The Collected Works of C.G. Jung. Vol 13.* Princeton University Press, (1969) Para 18.

CHAPTER 35 Awareness of Oneness of the Eternal 'I-I'

1. Venkataramiah, Munagala, S, *Talks with Sri Ramana Maharshi,* Sri Ramanasramam. (2013) Talks 265 p. 231-232

CHAPTER 36 Method and Truth

1. Venkataramiah, Munagala, S, *Talks with Sri Ramana Maharshi,* Sri Ramanasramam. (2013) Talks 363 p. 345-346

2. Ibid., *Talks* 188 p. 159

3. Ibid., *Talks* 338 p. 319

4. Ibid., *Talks* 354 p. 335-336

5. Ibid., *Talks* 503. p. 504

6. Ibid., *Talks* 618. P. 601

CHAPTER 37 The Alternative Method - The Path of Devotion

1. Venkataramiah, Munagala, S, *Talks with Sri Ramana Maharshi,* Sri Ramanasramam. (2013) Talks 363 p. 345-346

2. Mudaliar, Devaraja, *Day by Day with Bhagavan.* Sri Ramanasramam (2013) p. 266

3. Venkataramiah, Munagala, S, *Talks with Sri Ramana Maharshi,* Sri Ramanasramam. (2013) Talks 450 p. 440

CHAPTER 38 No Teacher is Necessary

1. Venkataramiah, Munagala, S.,*Talks with Sri Ramana Maharshi*, Sri Ramanasramam. (2013) Talk 282 p. 251

2. Ibid., *Talks* 434 p. 421

3. Sri Ramanasramam, *Who AM I? in The Collected Works of Ramana Maharshi*, (2001) 20

CHAPTER 39 Effort and Perseverance

1. Venkataramiah, Munagala, S, *Talks with Sri Ramana Maharshi*, Sri Ramanasramam. (2013) Talks 28 p. 30

2. Ibid., *Talks* 66 p. 44

3. Ibid., *Talks* 371 p. 351

4. Ibid., *Talks* 398 p. 384

5. Subbaramayya, G.V, *Sri Ramana Reminiscences*, Sri Ramanasramam. (2014) p. 156-157

CHAPTER 40 Reality and the Removal of the Unreal

1. Venkataramiah, Munagala, S, *Talks with Sri Ramana Maharshi*, Sri Ramanasramam. (2013) Talks 28 p.29-30

2. Venkataramiah, Munagala, S, *Talks with Sri Ramana Maharshi*, Sri Ramanasramam. (2013) Talks 446. p. 431-432

3. Venkataramiah, Munagala, S, *Talks with Sri Ramana Maharshi*, Sri Ramanasramam. (2013) Talks 33 p. 41-42

4. Swarnagiri, Ramanananda, *Crumbs from His Table.* Sri Ramanasramam (2017) p. 40)

5. Subbaramayya, G.V., *Sri Ramana Reminiscences,* Sri Ramanasramam
    (2014) p. 71

6. Venkataramiah, Munagala, S, *Talks with Sri Ramana Maharshi,*
    Sri Ramanasramam. (2013) Talks 487 p. 481- 483

7. Ibid., *Talks* 487 p. 484

8. Ibid., *Talks* 489 p. 486

9. Ibid., *Talks* 618 p. 602

10. Mudaliar, Devaraja, *Day by Day with Bhagavan.* Sri Ramanasramam
    (2013) p. 277

CHAPTER 41 Does Knowledge of Scriptures help?

1. Osborne, Arthur, The Rhythm of History, Indica Books (2011)

2. Venkataramiah, Munagala, S, *Talks with Sri Ramana Maharshi,*
    Sri Ramanasramam. (2013) Talks 226 p. 194

3. Ibid., *Talks* 230 p. 195

4. Mudaliar, Devaraja, *Day by Day with Bhagavan.* Sri Ramanasramam
    (2013) p. 265

CHAPTER 42 Limitations of the Intellect, Psychology and Analysis

1. Venkataramiah, Munagala, S, *Talks with Sri Ramana Maharshi,*
    Sri Ramanasramam. (2013) Talks 28 p. 31

2. Ibid., *Talks* 13 p.5-6

3. Cohen, S.S., *Guru Ramana Memories and Notes.* Sri Ramanasramam
    (2003) p. 58-59

4. Venkataramiah, Munagala, S, *Talks with Sri Ramana Maharshi*, Sri Ramanasramam. (2013) Talks 502 p. 499-500

5. Ibid., *Talks* 596 P. 569

6. Ibid., *Talks* 644 p. 622-623

7. Ibid., *Talks* 618 p. 601

8. Mudaliar, Devaraja, *Day by Day with Bhagavan*. Sri Ramanasramam (2013) p. 37

CHAPTER 43   Self-enquiry or Meditation

1. Venkataramiah, Munagala, S, *Talks with Sri Ramana Maharshi*, Sri Ramanasramam. (2013) Talks 390 p. 371-372

CHAPTER 44 Einstein's Genius as understood by Ramana Maharshi

1. Venkataramiah, Munagala, S, *Talks with Sri Ramana Maharshi*, Sri Ramanasramam. (2013) Talks 384 p. 364-365

2. Mudaliar, Devaraja, *Day by Day with Bhagavan*. Sri Ramanasramam (2013) p. 90

3. Venkataramiah, Munagala, S, *Talks with Sri Ramana Maharshi*, Sri Ramanasramam. (2013) Talks 193 p. 164-165

4. Ibid., *Talks* 209 p. 183-184

5. Ibid., *Talks* 426 p. 409-410

6. Mudaliar, Devaraja, *Day by Day with Bhagavan*. Sri Ramanasramam (2013) p. 266

7. B.V. Narasimha Swami, Ch. XXII *Self Realisation* (1937) p. 142-146

CHAPTER 45   Morality

1. Cohen, S.S., *Guru Ramana Memories and Notes.* Sri Ramanasramam (2003) p.47-48

2. Venkataramiah, Munagala, S, *Talks with Sri Ramana Maharshi,* Sri Ramanasramam. (2013) Talks 420 p. 404

3. Ibid., *Talks* 453. P. 444

4. Rumi, *A Great Wagon,* available at https://onbeing.org/poetry/a-great-wagon/, accessed 12 February 2025

CHAPTER 46   A life of Thought - Einstein's Legacy

1. *Einstein's Thought Experiments,* available at https://en.wikipedia.org/wiki/Einstein%27s_thought_experiments, accessed 16 January 2025

2. Caltech, *Einstein Papers Project, The Collected Papers of Albert Einstein.* Einstein and Mach: Creating History and Philosophy of Physics as a Discipline, available at https://www.einstein.caltech.edu/news/einstein-and-mach-creating-history-and-philosophy-of-physics-as-a-discipline#:~:text=Mach%20sided%20with%20Leibniz%20against,was%20also%20a%20relative%20matter, accessed 16 January 2025

3. Storr, Anthony, *The Dynamics of Creation,* Pelican, (1972) p. 90

4. Vallentin, Antonia. *Einstein.* London: Weidenfeld & Nicolson.(1965) p. 9.

5. Einstein, Albert, *The Collected Papers of Albert Einstein,* Princeton University Press. (2005), available at https://einsteinpapers.press.princeton.edu/, accessed 28 January 2025

6. Kessler, Harry. Dinner conversation between Alfred Kerr and Einstein recorded in, *The Diary of a Cosmopolitan* (1971)June 14, 1927.

CHAPTER 47   A life of Being Still - Ramana Maharshi's Legacy

1. Sri Ramanasramam, *The Collected Works of Ramana Maharshi*, (2001)

2. Venkataramiah, Munagala, S, *Talks with Sri Ramana Maharshi*, Sri Ramanasramam. (2013) Talks 453 p. 444

CHAPTER 48 Compassion

1. 4. https://www.youtube.com/watch?v=Q4K5IzjJK-k

2. Osborne, Arthur, *Ramana Maharshi and the Path of Self-knowledge*, Sri Ramanasramam (2012) p. 128

3. Ibid., *Ramana Maharshi and the Path of Self-knowledge,* p. 138

4. Subramanian S. Hari Hara, *Sri Ramana, Friend of the Animals. The Life of Cow Lakshmi*, (2004]

5. Osborne, Arthur, *Ramana Maharshi and the Path of Self-knowledge*, Sri Ramanasramam (2012] p. 133

6. Ibid., *Ramana Maharshi and the Path of Self-knowledge,* p. 128

CHAPTER 49 The End

1. Osborne, Arthur, *Ramana Maharshi and the Path of Self-knowledge*, Sri Ramanasramam (2012] p. 222

CHAPTER 50 Epilogue

1. Nimenko, Wasyl. *The Jackal: Young and Old. Reminiscences of Narikutti Swami*. Mountain Path (2012) Vol 49 No. 3 p. 49-56 Sri Ramanasramam., available at https://www.gururamana. org/Resources/mountain-path, accessed 28 January 2028

2. Wikipedia, *Santha Swami,* Available at https://aryasangha.org/ yogaswami.htm, accessed 28 January *2025*

3. Wikipedia, *Adrian Snodgrass,* available at *https://en.wikipedia.org/ wiki/Adrian_Snodgrass, accessed January 28 2025*

4. *"King of Lankapuri" : Sri Yoga Swami of Jaffna.* Mountain Path (1994) Vol 31 Nos. 3 and 4 p. 157-162, Sri Ramanasramam, available at https://www.gururamana.org/Resources/mountain-path, accessed 28 January 2028

5. Wikipedia, *Yoga Swami of Jaffna,* The Maharshi, May/june 2018 Vol 28. No.23, Available at https://archive.arunachala.org/ newsletters/2018/may-jun, accessed 28 January 2028

6. Yogaswami, *Natchintanai-* (2004) Thiruvadi

Notes on Chapters

Chapter 11, pages 40-45 are a transcript of, Nimenko W. (2018] *Virtual Reality and Sacred Places*. The Mountain Path, (2018) Vol 55 No, 4, Sri Ramanasramam. It also appeared in Nimenko Wasyl, *Notes from the Inside*, Chapter 29, Brigand London (2017)

Chapter 21, pages 75-76 are a transcript of chapter 3 in, Nimenko Wasyl, *Removing Our Delusion of Separateness*, Goalpath Books (2023)

Chapter 22, pages 78-81 are a transcript of chapter 6 in, Nimenko Wasyl, *Removing Our Delusion of Separateness*, Goalpath Books (2023)

Recommended Reading

Einstein

Isaacson, Walter, *Einstein, His Life and Universe*. Simon & Schuster UK Ltd (2007)

Jammer, Max, *Einstein and Religion*, Princeton (1999)

Dukas and Hoffman, Albert Einstein *The Human Side-Glimpses from His Archives*, Princeton (1979)

Ramana Maharshi

Sri Ramanasramam, *The Collected Works of Ramana Maharshi*, (2001)

Venkataramiah, Munagala. S., *Talks with Sri Ramana Maharshi*, Sri Ramanasramam. (2013)

Osborne, Arthur, *Ramana Maharshi and the Path of Self-knowledge*, Sri Ramanasramam (2012)

Bibliography

Arunachala, Sadhu, (Major A.W. Chadwick), *A Sadhu's Reminiscences of Ramana Maharshi,* Sri Ramanasramam (2005)

Brunton, Paul, *A Search in Secret India.* (1934)

Calaprice, Alice, *Dear Professor Einstein: Albert Einstein's Letters to and from Children.* Foreword by Evelyn Einstein. Amherst, N.Y.: Prometheus, (2002)

Calaprice, Alice, *The Ultimate Quotable Einstein,* Princeton University Press,(2011)

Cohen, S.S., *Guru Ramana Memories and Notes,* Sri Ramanasramam (2003)

Dukas and Hoffman, Albert Einstein *The Human Side-Glimpses from His Archives,* Princeton (1979)

Einstein, Albert, *Ideas and Opinions,* Crown Publishers, New York (1954)

Einstein, Albert, *On Cosmic Religion and Other Opinions & Aphorisms,* Covici-Friede, Inc New York (1931)

Einstein, Albert, *Out of my Later Years,* Philosophical Library New York (1950)

Einstein, Albert, *The Need for Ethical Culture,* in Mein Weltbild; Ideas and Opinion. (1954)

Einstein, Albert, *The Collected Papers,* The Digital Version https://einsteinpapers.press.princeton.edu/vol1-trans/

Frankl, Victor, *Mans Search For Meaning,* Rider, (2004)

Freud, Sigmund, *The Standard Edition of the Complete Psychological Works of Sigmund Freud*. The Hogarth Press and the Institute of Psychoanalysis (1964)

Gattegno, Caleb, *Silent Way*, Educational Solutions, Inc.,(1963)

Gordon-Brown, I. with Somers Barbara. *The Raincloud of Knowable Things*. (Archive Publishing, (2008)

Griffiths, Paul. J., *An Apology for Apologetics: A Study in the Logic of Interreligious Dialogue*. Wipf and Stock.(2007)

Highfield, Roger, Carter, Paul, *The Private Lives of Albert Einstein* Faber & Faber (1993)

Isaacson, Walter, *Einstein, His Life and Universe*. Simon & Schuster UK Ltd (2007)

Jammer, Max, *Einstein and Religion*, Princeton (1999)

Jung, C. G., *The Collected Works of C.G. Jung. Vol 11*. Princeton University Press,(1969)

Jung, C. G., *The Collected Works of C.G. Jung. Vol 13*. Princeton University Press,(1969)

Jung, C. G., Letters of C. G. Jung: Volume 2, 1951-1961, Routledge (1976)

Kessler, Harry. *The Diary of a Cosmopolitan*, (1971)

Mudaliar, Devaraja, *Day by Day with Bhagavan*, Sri Ramanasramam (2013)

Nagamma, Suri, *Letters from Sri Ramanasramam*, Sri Ramanasramam (1985)

Osborne, Arthur, *Ramana Maharshi and the Path of Self-knowledge*,

Sri Ramanasramam (2012)

Osborne, Arthur, The Rhythm of History, Indica Books (2011)

Osborne, Arthur, *The Teachings of Ramana Maharshi in His Own Words,* Sri Ramanasramam (2002)

Princeton University Press and the Hebrew University. *The Collected Papers of Albert Einstein, The Early Years,* 1879-1902 (English Translation Supplement]

Schilpp, Paul Arthur, (Ed.) 'Autobiographical Notes' in *Albert Einstein: Philosopher- Scientist, The* Library of Living Philosophers Volume VII (1970)

Shah, Idries, *The Elephant in the Dark,* Octagon Press (1974)

Shah, Idries,*The Exploits of the Incomparable Mulla Nasrudin,* Octagon Press (1966)

Sri Ramanasramam, *The Collected Works of Ramana Maharshi,* (2001)

Storr, Anthony, *The Dynamics of Creation,* Pelican, (1972)

Storr, Anthony, *Feet of Clay - A Study of Gurus,* Harper Collins, (1996)

Subbaramayya, G.V., *Sri Ramana Reminiscences,* Sri Ramanasramam. (2014)

Subramanian S. Hari Hara, *Sri Ramana, Friend of the Animals. The Life of Cow Lakshmi,* (2004)

Swami, B.V. Narasimha Ch. XXII *Self Realisation,* (1937)

Swarnagiri, Ramanananda, *Crumbs from His Table,*
Sri Ramanasramam (2017)

Tzu, Lau. *Tao Te Ching,* Gia-Fu Feng and Jane English. Vintage,
(1989)

Venkataramiah, Munagala. S., *Talks with Sri Ramana Maharshi,*
Sri Ramanasramam. (2013)

Viereck, George, *Glimpses of the Great,* Henrietta Street London
(1930)

Webster, Richard. *Why Freud was wrong: Sin, Science and
Psychoanalysis.* Orwell Press (1995)

Yogaswami, *Natchintanai,.* Thiruvadi Trust (2004)

211

Index

∞

Printed in Great Britain
by Amazon

60828457R00131